The World Is Not as We Think It Is

Dennis Littrell

This is for my grandsons, Kyle and Harrison, and for young people everywhere.

May you know the truth—the real truth, not the usual bromides put out by society—and may the truth set you free.

Table of Contents

A variation on the thought experiment
The same in everyone

Chapter Ten: The Paradox of Free Will

Swarm intelligence in the brain
The necessary illusion
Compatibilism
Quantum indeterminacy
Christianity
What causes a decision to be made?
Causation is also a mystery
Cognitive dissonance
Superorganisms

Chapter Eleven: Infinities

Beyond our ability to understand
So again does two plus two equal four?
Paradox
Some ideas are not fathomable
The probability field
Infinitely divisible

Chapter Twelve: Doubt and the 10,000 Things

Everything breaks down at the extremes
Mathematics is a language
Postmodern mathematics?
A yearning to divide by zero
The substantive "nothing"
Cartesian doubt
A subjective sense of what is agreeable
Deductive and inductive truths
The danger of absolute knowledge
Morality is a human construct

Chapter Thirteen: Nothing Is Real

Time

Introduction

"Know thyself," the oracle of Delphi urged; but can we truly know ourselves? Can the object of our contemplation gaze into the mirror and see itself objectively?

This book attempts to answer the question of who we are in light of both ancient and modern knowledge, especially the latter. My approach is skeptical, cynical and without consideration for political correctness.

I have been fortunate throughout most of my life with being able to spend a good part of my time reading and writing. In my youth I read a lot of fiction including most of the great masters of the 19th and 20th centuries, Twain, Tolstoy, Dostoevsky, Nabokov, Hesse, etc. I also read a lot of popular psychology. In my thirties I began to concentrate on science, especially cosmology, biology, ecology, physics and the history of science and mathematics. In the 1970s I began a life-long study of religion, especially Eastern religions while I practiced yoga on a daily basis. In the 1990s I discovered evolutionary psychology and spent some considerable time in becoming familiar with its growing literature. I have also been interested in philosophy. My main motivation has been self-study so I that I might better understand myself and my relationship with the world around me.

Self-study is not navel-gazing—although I have tried that. Self-study is the study of self in relation to our place in the cosmos. What I have learned is that we are not alone, that everything is connected, and that it is impossible to understand ourselves without understanding our relationships with others, with our culture and the other forms of life on this planet.

We live in symbiosis with those other forms of life. Without the amber fields of grain, the fish in the sea, the cows in the meadow, without the bacteria in our guts we would die. Without the oxygen in the air, made available and handed down to us by primeval microorganisms, we would not even exist. The vast wealth that we have today we owe to those who have gone before, those who built the cities, the roads, the farms, the homes we live in, the social organizations and the laws we follow.

I also learned that we cannot be understood through a reductive study of our anatomy or through a parsing of our genome. We are more than the atoms in our bodies and more than we can ever know.

No man is an island and we could not be explained to putative aliens in distant worlds without a recognition of all that surrounds us and our connection to all that surrounds us. As Franklin M. Harold phrased it in his book, *The Way of the Cell: Molecules, Organisms and the Order of Life* (2001): "...sending aliens the genome of a cat is no substitute for sending the cat itself—complete with mice." (p. 221)

So what this book is about is you, especially if you are relatively young and starting out in life. I want you to know *now* what I have spent decades learning, and I want to present this knowledge unvarnished, unadorned, without euphemism in the hope that you and all that you are connected to might profit from that knowledge.

The main lesson to be learned is that the world is not as we think it is, that we miss most of what is going on around us, and that there is much about ourselves we will never know.

Chapter One:

The Biological Imperatives

Sweet nothings...

—popular song lyric

Sex and subsistence

The first thing is to understand the biological imperatives, the most formidable of which are our dear friends, sex and subsistence.

Whether we know it or not, barring error we always act in accordance with one or the other or both of these imperatives. Sometimes the social need, which is really just a subsection of the sexual or subsistence imperative, causes us to act in discord with these needs and in accordance with the needs of others, the tribe, the society, usually because we have been indoctrinated or fooled and don't realize it.

These two imperatives dominate all our behavior and all the behaviors of everybody we know.

Whenever somebody calls you on the phone, texts you, whenever somebody takes an interest in you, whenever you are solicited in any way, it is for one or more of the following three reasons:

- They want to have a sexual/romantic/reproductive relationship with you. Call it sex.
- They want to bond with you or be your friend. Call it social.
- They want to trade with you (sell you something or buy something from you) or to work with you for a common economic purpose (or exploit you). Call it subsistence.

Everything is done for sex, for social reasons, or for subsistence. And by the way, subsistence means everything from a roof over your head to food and water to money in the bank to all worldly goods and services.

Self-deception

Consequently people will lie to you. And you will lie to them. This isn't exactly a bulletin. We all practice deception at times to get what we want. Sometimes we even practice self-deception.

I'm going to talk more than a bit about self-deception in this book because self-deception is integral to the way humans cope with the world. And we come by it honestly. Our ancestors early learned to deceive themselves in order to maintain *psychological homeostasis* (another term central to understanding what it is to be human).

Psychological homeostasis is similar to physiological homeostasis except that instead of maintaining a steady body temperature, a fairly consistent blood sugar level, oxygenation, etc., what we humans try to do is maintain an acceptable level of psychological comfort consistent with our self-image. No man considers himself a scoundrel (and no woman either, by the way); but sometimes we do bad things, cowardly things, hateful, despicable things, or maybe we just tell lies about our sex life or

17

how much we drink. To resolve the consequent *cognitive dissidence* and to maintain our image of ourselves as good guys and gals we don't admit we did bad things. No, what we do is tell ourselves that we really didn't actually cheat on our spouse because actually we didn't really feel anything for that person and furthermore we are going to eat less tomorrow so we didn't really overeat when you look at it from the standpoint of a two-day scenario. And so on.

A very readable book (with a great title!) that looks deeply into cognitive dissidence is *Mistakes Were Made (but not by me)* (2007) by Carol Tavris and Elliot Aronson.

Deceit is fundamental

...*[I]f (as Richard Dawkins argues) deceit is fundamental in animal communication, then there must be strong selection to spot deception and this ought, in turn, to select for a degree of self-deception, rendering some facts and motives unconscious so as not to betray—by the subtle signs of self-knowledge—the deception being practiced.*

—Robert L. Trivers, from the Foreword to the first edition of Richard Dawkins' *The Selfish Gene*.

Trivers adds, most insightfully, "Thus, the conventional view that natural selection favors nervous systems which produce ever more accurate images of the world must be a very naïve view of mental evolution." (p. xx in the third edition).

We can also call the deceitful mental gymnastics that humans practice "double think" as it was called in Orwell's *1984*, or simply hypocrisy. We will often observe blind deceit in the minds of those of a political party different from our own or in the minds of those who follow a religion different from our own. To spot hypocrisy in our own mind is a sometime thing, like seeing a black swan.

The irrational

But—and this often leads to trouble—sometimes what we do we do for irrational reasons. Sometimes we are being used unbeknownst to ourselves by the evolutionary mechanism, by others, by society, by organizations with their own agendas, by shamans, by tricksters, by exploiters, by General Motors and General Mills, by ayatollahs and the Reverends Bob Jones and Jerry Falwell, by Fox News Corp and Disney Productions, by Dr. Phil and Phillip Morris, by an insistent voice in our head that whispers seductively (while we're thinking of chocolate chip cookie dough ice cream): "You're worth it!"

If you are young, sex and social needs dominate and account for most of your activities and those of your peer group. And don't forget that. *That* is what *they* are up to. If you are in your middle years, most of your behavior and that of your colleagues is to further the bottom line and raise your children (or perhaps get something on the side). If you are old and retired nobody cares why you do things and you yourself are often confused about your motives or goals. Or maybe you're free. The main thing to understand is that when you're old, when people want a relationship with you nine times out of ten it is for purely economic reasons. If the persons interested in you are young, they probably are looking to take advantage of you in some way.

Don't let your relatives control you, don't let your friends control you, don't let society control you, and don't let the evolutionary mechanism control you.

A devil in the essence

But there is a devil in the essence, a trickster who keeps us from a strict determinism. This is the random or the playful or the inexplicable. In the quantum world some things cannot be known, momentum and position simultaneously, for example. Why your child likes to lick the cell phone, why your dog likes cats, why for no apparent reason at no particular juncture you make a mistake or amazingly enough do exactly the right thing—these behaviors are necessary because without variance in our actions we would be stagnant and not capable of evolving.

So add to the imperatives, mistakes, the nonessential, the random, the things we do seemingly for no reason at all. These behaviors too are built in.

Chapter Two:

The World Is Not as We Think It Is

Look out kid, they keep it all hid.

—Bob Dylan

The world is not as we think it is. In life there is a persistent quality of misapprehension that is next to impossible to dispel. In Zen and certain mystical approaches it is dispelled by "enlightenment." In our everyday lives it is dispelled occasionally by some sort of insight brought about by a confluence of events, usually something seemingly earth-shaking. The problem is that this enlightenment or insight is often just temporary and we forget the next day, or, like the thread of a dream dimly recalled, we lose the essence of the understanding that we had momentarily gained, and we are returned to the mundane world.

Dumbing us down

The reason for this is surprising: the forces of society and the evolutionary mechanism conspire to return us to ignorance since they "want" us to do their bidding. They don't want us to know too much otherwise we might act contrary to *their* needs. Consequently, the evolutionary mechanism uses hormones and brain chemistry to get you to do what it wants done. The society uses psychology, social pressure and various reward/punishment systems to get you to contribute to the success of society.

There is a sense in which we individual humans have gotten too bright for our own good, and the evolutionary mechanism has had to dumb us down lest our smarts get the better of our survival and reproductive imperatives. We see this in our belief in an afterlife and in the ovulation of women which is hidden from us.

Hidden ovulation

Consider that men do not consciously know when the woman is ovulating. There are no outward signs. The woman herself usually does not know. Why should this be? A quick answer is that it would not be adaptive for humans to know.

Consider that if the woman were certain about when she was ovulating she might avoid sex at that time so as not to become pregnant allowing her to avoid having to deal with all the consequences of pregnancy, one of which until modern times was the very real possibility of dying while giving birth. Further consider that if the man knew when the woman was and was not ovulating he would be there by her side when ovulating and elsewhere when she wasn't. There would be no "mate guarding" and she would have trouble keeping him around to help with the kids. This is *not* what the evolutionary mechanism wants for humans.

Similarly our belief in an afterlife is in part a direct consequence of our conscious knowledge that we will die. Fear of death in other animals is an immediate and instinctive reaction. They do not fear their death tomorrow. But we do. We know we are going to die, and to keep this knowledge from making life meaningless, which may cause us to struggle less to survive and reproduce, we believe in an afterlife which gives us the strength to go on.

The truth of who we are is hidden from us

We do not know who we are, but we know enough to know we are not who we think we are.
—Pierre Baldi, from *The Shattered Self: The End of Natural Evolution*, p. xiii)

The truth of our lives and who we are is deliberately hidden from us by not only society and the evolutionary mechanism, but by most of the institutions of society, including our churches, synagogues, ashrams and schools, even our parents. They have their agendas and they keep it all hid. Our task is to push aside the veil of illusion and see life and ourselves as we really are, not as society, other people, or the evolutionary mechanism would have us believe.

Four masters

The imperatives of the evolutionary force are often in conflict because the evolutionary force wants you to survive, but it also wants you to reproduce as effectively and as often as practical. Society is interested in using you for its purposes, and your parents want you to make them look good, to give meaning to their lives or possibly to provide vicarious experiences for them. Consequently it can be said that we have four masters. We are in bondage to these masters, and the purpose of life—if life has a purpose—is to free ourselves from this bondage. We are in bondage to:

- Our need to find subsistence.

- The biological imperative to reproduce.

- The need to be social.

- The requirements of self or homeostasis, both physical homeostasis and psychological homeostasis.

All human activities can be grouped under one or more of these headings. The trick is to free ourselves in so far as possible from these masters. This is the goal of enlightenment.

Being free

And remember, you don't have to go along with the evolutionary mechanism's program or that of society. You can be not antisocial but unsocial. You can be *not* self-destructive, but *non*-reproductive. It is good to live within the sea of the society but be not of the society. It is good to go along with the ways and means of society but with loyalty not to society but to oneself. As Kipling said,

If you can walk with crowds and keep your virtue,
Or walk with Kings—nor lose the common touch,
If neither foes nor loving friends can hurt you,
If all men count with you, but none too much;
If you can fill the unforgiving minute
With sixty seconds' worth of distance run,
Yours is the Earth and everything that's in it,
And—which is more—you'll be a Man, my son!

Or a woman, as you like.

Chapter Three:

Our Reality Is Inside Our Heads

Reality is a mass hallucination.

—Howard Bloom, *Global Brain: The Evolution of Mass Mind from the Big Bang to the 21st Century* (2000), p. 193

We need logical argument and evidence. But we also need music and poetry. We need parables. We need story, myth and magic. We have to somehow circumvent the limbic system. The rational mind is not capable of that since it is the slave of the limbic system. The limbic system, the mammalian brain, the reptilian brain, etc., can be seduced and persuaded by poetry, by story and song, even by ideas and brute facts, but only occasionally by rational argument. And so various verbal techniques must be employed.

Solid objects are not solid. If we could see objects as they are we might see the tiniest bits or clouds of energy amidst huge amounts of empty space. Such objects feel hard and impenetrable because that is the way it is handy for us to feel them and to see them. This is an example of the world not being the way we think it is. Consider that the earth could be compressed into an object too small for us to see; and the entire universe supposedly existed very early on somewhere near the size of the Planck limit which is something like 1.6 times ten to the minus 35th, which is too small for humans to comprehend.

Our reality is something we superimpose on the world, crafted for us by the evolutionary mechanism. In fact our reality is inside our heads. We see what we need to see, hear what avails us, and feel, touch and taste in a way that furthers our existence and ability to reproduce. Anything extraneous to subsistence or sex is ignored by the evolutionary mechanism.

The illusive nature of perception

Consequently there is an illusive quality about our perception of the world that cannot be dispelled. This fact was known to the ancients in the East and has been rediscovered by the moderns in the West. The reason for the difference between the world and our perception of it has to do with the fact that the evolutionary mechanism did not hone us to perceive the truth of nature, but instead fashioned us to see the world in a way that furthered our survival.

In most cases the best way to insure our survival was to allow us to see the world as it "objectively" is, that is, as pure instruments might see it. There are exceptions however, because sometimes to see the world objectively is not adaptive (recall the need to maintain psychological homeostasis); and in other cases there is no advantage in seeing the world as it really is. For example we do not see ultraviolet light. There is no adaptive advantage for our doing so, or at least any advantage is so small as not to matter. For bees and certain birds, that do see ultraviolet light, there is an advantage in doing so.

Our limited perceptional ability

Furthermore we see only a very small part of what there is to see. We cannot see microorganisms, although they are everywhere. We can't smell the myriad odors that waft around us. There is a whole world of scents full of information that we can't appreciate, a world of beauty and wonder probably equal to or even surpassing that which we experience with our eyes. We can't see the air that envelops us as the water envelops the creatures of the sea. We do not always notice the lies that other people tell us, such as the shamans and priests and our glorious leaders, because to do so would lessen the survival of the tribe; and we are so intimately wedded to our tribe, our band, our family, our nation that without them we could not survive. And indeed most of us probably wouldn't want to.

Additionally, our conscious minds are only aware of a very small part of what our senses are experiencing. There is no evolutionary reason for our conscious minds to be aware of everything that is going on, and in fact such knowledge would only overwhelm us to no good effect; indeed too much knowledge of a nonessential nature would be counterproductive. So the bandwidth of consciousness excludes much of the nonessential. Consequently we experience consciously only a very small part of what it is possible to experience.

We experience only conceptual objects

Physicist/philosopher Martin G. Walker in his book, *Life! Why We Exist... And What We Must Do to Survive* (2006) explains that we do not experience the world directly; the objects that we see and touch are *conceptual objects*, not the objects themselves. He explains that conceptual objects are sufficiently like physical objects for our purposes as evolutionary beings. Our perceptions are utilitarian, one might say. A brown chair is brown although in fact it is white with light in some places and dark with shadow in others because it is a conceptual chair that we see, and we miss the subtleties that do not relate to the chair's utility as a discrete object (unless of course we are artists). We do this with everything in the world because it would be far too complex (and of little or no evolutionary value) to see things more precisely.

What we do see, hear, feel, taste and smell we construct in our minds. What John Locke called the secondary qualities of objects such as color, sound and taste exist as experiences in our minds quite apart from what pure instruments might experience. Furthermore we see only a small range of electromagnetic radiation and we hear only a small range of sounds. We smell very little of what there is to smell. Our view is clouded and conditioned by our biological needs.

Perception follows biological need

Our view of the world is illusive because our perception is so massively ordered by our needs and our beliefs. A personal, anthropomorphic God and an afterlife are very real to most people. Ghosts and angels, devils and little green men are part of the world of most people. Little animals are cute because they are non-threatening and might serve in an emergency as dinner. Shit stinks and is ugly and avoided because of the danger of pathogens. Women are beautiful or not based on our perception of their fertility based on standards built into our psyches, and so on and on. Even greenery and waterways are beautiful because of their utility.

Furthermore we are stuck in a certain time frame of observational experience. We cannot experience very short frames of time or very long ones. We see only a very small part of what there is to see. We don't see bacteria or the air (usually). We are always looking for psychological homeostasis and therefore the "truth" of what we see and how we experience not only the natural world but other people is based on how our perceptions protect our egos, and indeed we distort reality to protect our egos. We rationalize our behavior and selectively recall what we have and have not done, so that our experience of the past is further distorted. We selectively hear what we want to hear or what we expect to hear. We even see, feel, and taste in a way that is distorted by our expectations or desires.

To a cat the world is gray and full of scents and movements. To a dog it is a mass of scents and sounds that we experience only fractionally.

When a bird is looking for a place to nest it is guided by instinct. It may fly by possible spots and then perch in a likely place. It judges the spot on how it *feels*. If it is made to feel uncomfortable, it moves on. We do the same sort of thing, but the difference is that we are sometimes (not always by any means) aware of the process. And of course we can direct ourselves consciously toward such behavior.

The brain, the body, our ideas, our "natural" prejudices, the extent and limit of what we can see, hear, and even imagine are shaped by the necessity to survive. We see only what we need to see. I look about this room and I see windows and a floor, walls and ceiling, bookcases and I can make out individual books and even some of the words in the titles. But I cannot see the bacteria. Imagine a creature with the need the see the bacteria. How would its eyes work? I imagine it scanning a surface and with super microscopic vision see the colonies of bacteria come into view. How slowly would it have to move its head! Or more likely how different the vision modules of its brain would work. Perhaps it could process the visual information so fast that it would seem like a blur to us.

What color would the bacteria be? Color, as Locke had it, is a secondary quality, not present in the thing itself. The colors we experience are inside our heads not in the objects. There is no objective world out there independent of experience because how the world really *is* is a cooperative effort between viewer and viewed. To us the leaves on a tree are various shades of green allowing the orange fruits stand out. To a cat the leaves are gray and so are the oranges. A cat never eats an orange so the cat doesn't need to see it against the leaves. The cat needs to see small movements on the ground that might be made by rodents. So our brains are products of the evolutionary process, fashioned to serve our evolutionary needs.

We are not separate from the rest of the universe

I watch the red-shouldered hawk that sometimes perches in the tree outside my window. He scans the ground, his head able to twirl all the way around. I know his eyesight is better than mine. He can see little creatures on the ground. Suddenly I notice he has turned and is looking directly at me. I am inside behind the glass sliding door looking at him through binoculars. He stares directly at me for a moment. I imagine that he is irritated. This has happened before. Red-shouldered hawks do not like to be stared at. If you walk by a tree in which they are perched and just glance up and walk on without staring, everything is fine. Should you stop and stare, or worse, look at them through binoculars, they take off leaving one or two irritated cries behind, sounding something like a "caw" from a crow but higher pitched.

I imagine that before there were guns, before there were arrows or men to throw rocks, red-shouldered hawks did not mind being stared at as they perched comfortably out of reach.

We also don't see x-rays or, as some have pointed out, do philosophy very well. We are wonderful creatures when things go well for us, but should we not get what we need or desire or think we need, we can become ugly in the extreme. We will make behavioral exceptions for ourselves and justify them no matter how horrendous. We see green trees and hear running water and this pleases us because such an environment suggests comfort and is relatively full of things to eat. We feel affection for small furry animals, and birds. They are non-threatening, and truth to be told, might well serve us as a living storage of emergency rations. Everything we experience is colored by our evolutionary needs, or as I like to say, our need for sex and subsistence.

It's all intertwined. It's important to understand that. We don't end at the level of our skin. We don't begin with a homunculus in our brains.

A human being is a part of the whole, called by us "Universe," a part limited in time and space. He experiences himself, his thoughts and feelings as something separated from the rest, a kind of optical delusion of his consciousness.

—Albert Einstein, as quoted on ThinkExist.com.

Chapter Four:

How to Exploit the Opposite Sex
(and why you should)

The biological burden

This may seem a bit crass but before we can hope to form a mutually beneficial relationship we need to understand how to exploit the opposite sex and how we might be exploited, which is what often happens.

We will begin with the nature of women since they are the default sex. A population of humans might exist indefinitely with a lot fewer males, but it cannot maintain if there are few females. Naturally nature has taken care that neither a shortage of females nor males is possible for very long. It is true there are more males conceived and born than females, but it is also true that more males than females manage to kill themselves off before reaching maturity. Furthermore, as the population ages the percentage of females increases. We'll skip over the reasons for this for now.

The most important thing to understand about women is that they have a greater reproductive burden than men have. This biological difference has significant consequences, not the least of which is that females must be more careful in choosing with whom to have sex and especially with whom to marry. If there is a chance of becoming pregnant most women cannot afford casual sex. The penalty for casual sex (putting sexually transmitted diseases aside) can be high for women but of course rather low for men, which is why men are more promiscuous than women.

The alpha male

So far, so obvious. But what's a woman to do? Never forget that every woman on this planet comes from an unbroken line of women who got pregnant and delivered. From this we can conclude that women are very strongly driven to get pregnant and have children, which means they want to fuck—but they want to fuck the right man at the right time.

Who is that man and when is the right time?

The right man is the alpha male of the society. The alpha male of the society is strong, healthy, and has resources. He is usually confident (as well he should be) and he might be attractive, intelligent and even funny as well. But above all he must be strong, healthy and have resources.

For the woman two problems present themselves in finding and obtaining the services of this alpha male. First she must be sure that he is indeed an alpha male, and second that she can secure his services for a period of time sufficient to get her through pregnancy, breast feeding and beyond. Always keep in mind that although the woman wants to be fucked, at least by the alpha male, she wants more than sexual services. Wham-bam, thank you m'am, will not suffice for her, not by a long shot.

By the way, remember I am talking about the prehistory. Things have changed quite a bit since then, but our instincts are the same, and our instincts drive our behavior.

Flashing resources

Discerning the alpha male is relatively easy for most women. They can tell at a glance if a man is healthy and strong. Finding out if he has resources may take a bit longer, but that again is something that women are very good at. They have to be because many men are good at faking alpha male qualities, especially confidence and (in the modern Western world at least) the perception of resources. Flashing status is the way men attempt to influence female choice. Status implies resources. If you drive an expensive car, have a house on the hill, wear expensive clothes, have money to burn, etc., it's fairly clear you have the resources to support her and any children that might come along. Women do indeed get excited about flashes of wealth, as well they should. Bear in mind this preference for guys with resources is hard-wired into the female brain whether she admits it or not or even whether she knows it or not.

The obvious problem for the woman is the fact that there is a distinct shortage of alpha males and so the vast majority of women have to settle for lesser males. This is all sorted out long before they become women. Assessing their ability to attract males is something females begin doing as children. By the time they are in their teens most have something close to an unerring feel for the kind of male they can get and keep. Of course we all fool ourselves a lot, and some women are always reaching too high and some others settle for less than they could get.

The primordial need for a male

One thing to keep in mind here is that almost any male is better than no male at all—that is, it was in the prehistory. In most of today's societies women can get along quite well without a man. But because that was next to impossible during the long, long prehistory, women again have it hard-wired into their psyches that they have to have a man. In the prehistory, and sadly still in some societies today, a woman alone is in an unstable situation, a kind of vacuum that must be filled. In some Arab Muslim lands a woman cannot even go about in public without the escort of a male. Why? Because when a man sees a woman alone he is psychologically compelled to fill that perceived vacuum. No woman in the prehistory could exist without the protection of men—of course she was being protected from *other men*. Bonded males collectively consider women as something close to commodities and will use them as chattel unless there are otherwise prevented by law and custom.

A woman instinctively knows that being without a male makes her vulnerable to exploitation and that is one of the reasons she wants a man, and one of the reasons she wants the best man she can get. The omega male, the little boy nerd, the socially, politically and financially inept male is much like no male at all. The big boys will just kick sand in his face so to speak and he won't be able to do anything about it.

But it's more than just size. Size matters (of course) but consider that our human brains grew big and smart to deal with our complex social lives. This is the current wisdom. Socializing is a lot of work. We needed to be really smart to outsmart the other guy (or gal). We needed to be smart to juggle all those intrigues, social, political and sexual. I like the way this insight fits with the female's abhorrence of nerds: the fact of the matter is, not being social is also not being smart! So there, nerds!

Falling in love

Most women have to compromise, and most women end up with lesser males. Again what's a woman to do? If you are an alpha male (or have even been one, ha, ha) you know that a woman with a lesser male is usually easy pickings. This is evidence of the woman's overall strategy for exploiting males. Her predicament is dire; her options are limited. She has to have a male, she has to reproduce and she has to reproduce in a manner that gets her children to maturity so that they can reproduce. In fact the human female goes further than that: she helps to ensure that her grandchildren reach maturity so that they can reproduce.

Here's how she does it. She makes herself as attractive as possible. (Men judge women on attractiveness mainly because attractiveness signals good health. In the long run physical and mental health *is* what makes a woman attractive, never forget that. It's not lipstick that does it.) She carefully chooses the best provider from those she attracts—or actually she "falls in love" with the best of the limited choices she has. I put "falls in love" in quotation marks because this is the key for her. If she is in love then the choice is the right one. This state of being in love is the way her unconscious system directs her to the best choice she has considering her circumstances. The evolutionary mechanism isn't going to sit around and wait for Mr. Right. Time flies, the bird is always on the wing. We do not have the poet's "world enough and time." In the prehistory, the choice was made (or made for her) very near the time of her sexual maturity. In today's world the choice is typically put off until later. In either case she falls in love, hopefully with the guy she marries.

The need for intimacy

Once the woman identifies the best male she can get, she seeks intimacy. Intimacy is a technique that women instinctively develop in order to have some control over the relationship. Some men instinctively resist intimacy because they (unconsciously, of course) know that intimacy makes them lose some control of the relationship. If all you want is sex—and if you're an alpha male with a lesser female—you have no reason to allow intimacy. You should fake intimacy, but to really allow the woman into your heart of hearts is to give her too much information and too much emotional control.

If a woman cannot develop intimacy with the man she will probably fall out of love with him. Some women foolishly settle for something less than intimacy. They often pay the price, which usually comes in the form of being a single parent.

If the woman falls in love and develops intimacy with the man she will usually want to marry him and have children. This is what it is all about for the woman at this stage of her life. At this relatively brief point in her life even a very attractive alpha male will get turned down. Usually. The woman has what she wants and needs and the attentions of an alpha male at this time would just spoil things.

Cuckolding the male

However after some period of time—some call it the seven year itch, but I think the evidence suggests something like two to four years—the woman will be receptive to approaches from other males, especially if they are alpha males or at least superior to one she has. The woman can't help herself because this is part of the strategy built into her brain, mind, heart, soul, and body. The idea is to upgrade the genetic input. If she can success-fully cuckold her man (and something like ten to twenty percent of children born to married couples are not the children of the father) she will have the best of both worlds: a man who provides the resources necessary for her to raise her children and the best genes she can get as well.

"Nowhere lives a woman true and fair" advised the poet John Donne many years ago. (He might have just said "true" and left it at that since few women are so un-attractive as to not be able to give it away.) And it is true for even the most desirable women in the highest stations. The temptation to "cheat" is always there and often una-voidable. We used to think that many species of birds, like humans, formed bonds for life. But DNA evidence has shown that some of those eggs were fertilized by a bird other than the female bird's mate.

I said "unavoidable." Well that is not strictly true, is it? Many women go through life never cheating on their spouses. There are millions of women who have slept with only one man, and some of them have been sorely tempt-ed. Why haven't they strayed?

Well, social custom, the law (in some places), the fear of being ostracized, fear of her husband's anger, a cold calculation of possible gain and loss, lack of oppor-tunity, lack of suitable males, a strong belief that adultery is wrong, etc.

Men instinctively know that their mates may cheat which is why we have "mate guarding," chastity belts, and in some societies even today a kind of dictatori-al control of the movements of women. It may seem ironic that women are the ones who are less trusted, when of course men (as we will see) are to be trusted even less! The reasons are several, and we'll get to them shortly.

What do you want from the woman?

But for now, let's look a little deeper into the situation as it exists for women and see how we as able-bodied males might take advantage.

First what is our goal with women? Here are four possibilities:

1) Sex, pure and simple.
2) Wife and "helpmeet."
3) Worker, maid, servant, go-fer, in short, we want the woman's labor.
4) Her money.

In the case of sex, the challenge ranges from easy to effectively speaking impossible. To be blunt Jackie Kennedy does not spread her legs for Joe Six-Pack. A slightly overweight, emotionally-neglected plain Jane is easy pickings for even a less than average male if he has an inkling of how to go about his business. In between Mrs. Onassis and a Jerry Springer reject there are countless women waiting to be exploited. But a man has to make a living. He may have a wife and kids to provide for. His time and energy are limited. So what's a man to do?

The alpha male has his problems too

Let's begin with you as a single young man of modest means, average in most respects. Well, for illustrative purposes, let's first imagine that you are an alpha male in the prime of his life, meaning you are about 38 years old with a secure financial situation ("rich"). You are tall and handsome, refined with obvious social and political skills, charming, well-educated and sophisticated. You are the most interesting man in the world!

For sex—well, you have to fight them off. You actually have to be very careful about the women you have relationships with because they will want more—more of you, your time, and your resources, and that's even if you are a lousy lover. Ironically you might be wise to be as circumspect in your sexual behavior as Caesar's wife was advised to be. You will have to be a good judge of character and pick your liaisons carefully. Look at what happened to Tiger Woods and innumerable congressmen, senators, reverends, etc. It might be best to just have a wife and a mistress and settle for that.

As for a wife, well, you choose the healthiest, the smartest, the most beautiful, the most accomplished, the most loyal, the best educated, the most understanding, the wisest, the hardest working, the woman with the highest station in life...etc., or merely (and foolishly) follow your heart's desire. Following your heart of course is risky. This is in fact where the alpha male is the most vulnerable and where he can end up as the exploited. I won't go any further but refer the interested reader to the daily news.

As worker, servant, go-fer, etc., just hire somebody and keep your dick in your pants.

As for money, well, if your priority is to increase your resources, I will refer the interested reader to the lives of kings. Marrying for money is a risky business mainly because you are putting her resources (which you really don't need) above all the qualities mentioned above as reasons for marrying. Be careful.

The beta male's task

Okay, now that we have given you a glimpse of the alpha male's problems, let's see how you as that single young man of average or slightly above average attainment and stature—we'll call you a "beta male"—goes about getting the most for his effort.

If you just want sex, you're in good shape. Being young is what sex is all about. Or maybe I should say that sex is what being young is all about. And in today's world all the societal and practical difficulties of old associated with just getting fucked are greatly reduced. Dude, you don't live in the best of all possible worlds but you do live in the best one yet to arrive on his planet, sexually speaking.

First you need to make yourself as attractive as possible. As above we know that "attractive" for women begins with resources. (Being tall and handsome is a nice bonus.) In other words if you can make her believe you have lots of money and property you are home free. Of course you can't so what you do is put a lot of what you have into first impression type things like the most expensive car you can afford, the nicest clothes, a hairdresser, and you take her to the nicest places you can afford and no cheap hotels.

As stupid and obvious as this is it still works with a lot of women. They know you are an asshole who wastes what little time, energy, resources and skills he has on sexual exploits, but that's okay since she is probably isn't much herself and is in need of a fantasy. For many people at this time of their lives, sex is sex and they all look the same standing on their heads. Or something like that.

Note well that in the resource department you won't fool many women for very long. As far as personal qualities such as charm, intelligence, education, wit, etc., goes (yours) you'll have trouble faking them at all. The average woman (which is what the average guy can expect) will be a bit ahead of the average guy in the sizing up department. Remember the stakes are higher for her, so she has to be better.

The omega male's task

If you are below average (an omega male) in resources, charm, intelligence, looks, height, etc., you will have to work harder and maybe even...well, beg. You will have to learn to spot the most vulnerable and play to their vulnerabilities, provide them with booze, drugs, or whatever it is they need. As a not very desirable male you have to take what you can get and that will almost certainly mean less desirable females.

If nothing else you can develop sexual technique and built a reputation as a "sixty-minute man" who knows what he is doing and is "caring." If you are involved in a social circle where word gets around, you will have no trouble getting more than your fair share of sex. But it can be hard work and there's a learning curve.

Again: life isn't fair

Okay, forget about this sex only business. You are ready to settle down and you want the best helpmeet for life that you can find.

The first thing to understand is that if she seems just so cute and just so sexy and just so adorable, what that probably means is she has the ability to exploit *you*. If you have nothing to exploit, that is fine: follow your heart, fall madly in love and learn to mend a broken heart because that is what you are likely to get. She will either always keep you at a distance while she looks for someone better whom she will marry, or she will just reject you out of hand. You will be wise enough as an average young guy to know that you have no chance with beautiful, rich women. Sorry about that but as you know life isn't fair.

In the final analysis what you really need as an average Joe is somebody whose talents compensate for your weaknesses. You need somebody whose weaknesses are things you can put up with, and somebody who can live with your shortcomings. In other words, this is the give and take that the vast majority of humans in the modern societies have to work through as they try to find a mate. If you are careful and choose wisely you can get a bargain. More often you'll get a woman with some glaring faults that you'll just have to live with. But here's the good part, if she loves you, you do indeed have something wonderful, and if you love her too, it is beyond wonderful for as long as it lasts, which as stated above is for two to three, possible seven years, or in rare cases for life!

Male vs. female

All of this leads to differing views on how men see women and how women see men. From a male point of view women are crazy. What women do is self-destructive. Take the use of the word "fuck" as illustrative. To be fucked is to lose, to be taken advantage of, to be put in an unenviable position, to be defeated in some sense. You are "fucked over," you are "fucked up," you "got fucked," etc. Yet the blatant denotative meaning of the verb "to fuck" refers to the sexual act. We can tell however from the way the word is used in its multifarious ways that getting fucked is not good. Since women desire to be fucked and to allow a foreign entity (the fetus) to take over their bodies which will reduce their mobility and their ability to hunt and gather or fight off wild beasts, men just naturally think this is crazy, masochistic even.

From a female point of view men are stupid. They have these often injurious "competitions" among themselves to show who is stronger or smarter or more willing to risk life and limb. And to what purpose? To demonstrate to the female which among them is more likely to excite her fancy? From a woman's point of view it would be more to the point to just let her decide. She has eyes and can see. And as to the war system practiced by men, it is just insane. If the war system didn't exist, however, men would be less valuable than women. So the only way men can avoid being inferior to women is to have the war system. Since women are not the equal of men physically or in terms of reckless aggression, men will win the wars, or the tribe with the best men will win the wars. Such is stupidity, a woman will tell you.

Hell is other people

Every man should be king of the castle and every woman queen. Or every man and every woman should be absolute dictator of all aspects of their lives. In an ideal world we would all be kings and queens and princes and fairy princesses, and all our desires would be satisfied, except such desires as would be harmful. We would have near perfect knowledge of who we are and what we need to do at any given moment to maximize our happiness and sense of worth and self-respect. And someday this may happen. The technology to achieve such a state is many years in the future of course at best and of course even with the best engineering, humans may not be capable of reaching this ideal state. Or perhaps such is not the ideal state.

I mention this because usually the greatest obstacles to happiness in today's world are other people. Yes, other people. Whether those people are heads of state, terrorists, CEOs of international corporations, your next door neighbors, your friends and relatives, your spouse, they can bring pain, and they often do. In the future all the people we know will be virtual people and they will all behave admirably. Until then the best that we can do is avoid incompatible, negative and harmful people.

Feminism

At this point I want to add a few words about feminism. From one point of view feminism is a political and social movement designed to improve the status of women in the world vis-à-vis men. From another point of view feminism is just sexism. There is no "masculinism" since that is obviously politically incorrect and sexist. You never see this pointed out because the pat answer is that the world, as it is, is a form of masculinism and there is no need for a movement to improve the status of men. End of discussion.

From still another point of view there is the battle of the sexes—and which is to be master?

Two questions that might be asked are:

(1) Are women really worse off than men?
(2) If so, what can be done about it?

As to (1) surprisingly there can be some debate. Men die earlier and more often than women. Men have to endure things that women don't have to endure—combat, the salt mines, etc. (For more on this point of view see *The Myth of Male Power: Why Men Are the Disposable Sex* (1993) by Warren Farrell.)

Nonetheless the generally accepted answer is yes, women are worse off than men, especially in the Middle East and in the developing world overall. Whether women are worse off in the West today is less clear. They don't make as much money per capita as men, but there are reasons for that, mainly because most women often feel that they have better things to do than to work slavishly for the corporation. Also because from a corporate point of view a woman has a chance of becoming pregnant and diverting her energy away from the corporation, they are paid less. In this sense hiring a woman is a bit more of a risk for the corporation than hiring a man, and consequently it's only reasonable to pay her less.

As to (2), there is plenty that can be done about it, but is that enough? Biology is destiny to some very real extent. Men do not have wombs and therefore do not have babies and therefore will always have an easier time of it with regards to reproduction. But sex is not exactly gender and a lot of what is biased against women in the world is the result of what might be called genderization. Girls in pink dresses; women in high heels. The real problem is to define and recognize where sex ends and gender begins. There are hundreds perhaps thousands of courses in our colleges and universities that are defining and re-defining this problem every day.

Sexual selection

The inequality that we see in the world is not the fault of men per se or of women. It is built into the biological nature of human beings and can only be overcome by first understanding why the bias is there and realizing that both sexes have to work together to change things, just as both sexes form the species and work together to create the reality we experience in the first place.

This is a reality that we have experienced since before we were human. The stark ironic fact of the matter is that through sexual selection women have molded men and men have molded women. Women have breasts and other physical and psychological characteristics because men selected those characteristics in the women they preferentially chose to raise children with. Men are aggressive and often violent because in the past that has worked and women have preferentially chosen aggressive and violent men to mate with because they are the ones who had the best chance of gaining resources and being around to help raise the children. Women have not usually had the luxury of choosing nice guys who famously finish last. Ask a woman who she would prefer to have as a mate, Saddam Hussein or a weakling nerd, and you'll get a pause before she answers. Best answer, by the way, is "Are those the only choices?" Unfortunately sometimes those *are* the only choices. The woman who answered "weakling nerd" didn't raise many children.

We are stuck with our biological natures. The trick is to rise above biology. To some large extent civilization and the rule of law have allowed and are allowing us to do just that.

Fear of being cuckolded

As to the so-called battle of the sexes, it is very real (as outlined above). Humans have sexual strategies for reproduction (mostly unconscious) and in acting out these strategies men try to exploit exploitable women and vice-versa. In fact, you would not go far wrong by looking at every male-female relationship in terms of exploitation. Some men are vulnerable to some women. Such men will cater to and take care of such women. Some women are vulnerable to some men. Famously most women will just lie down for someone they perceive as the alpha male. They will take his genetic input and do their best to take care of the resulting child even if that requires exploiting another male. This is why, evolutionarily speaking, men are terrified of being cuckolded. Fear of being cuckolded and a fanatical desire to control paternity is in part what created the Middle Eastern religions (and some others) and allowed them to flourish.

Fear of being cuckolded stems directly from biology. Since the woman is never in doubt as to maternity, she doesn't have to worry about being cuckolded. (She has plenty of other worries of course.) The crude defense to being cuckolded that most societies came up with was to control women. Women are not so easy to control and so it sometimes took draconian measures to prevent women from exercising choice. Conservative expressions of Christianity, Judaism, Islam, Hinduism, etc., still seek to control women, and in many countries do so severely.

Women in control of men?

Still another question that might be asked is, is there a danger that women will end up in control of men? And if so, what would such a world be like? Would it be better or worse than the one that exists today?

Perhaps first it would be a good idea to ask why men got the upper hand in the first place. One would think that the sexes would be equal. To understand why patriarchy triumphed over matriarchy (or actually why matriarchy never arose in the first place except in isolated circumstances) we turn to the war system.

Chapter Five:

The War System

Killing members of our own group is murder, but killing members of other groups is the fastest way for a male to gain social prestige.

—William C. Burger, *Perfect Planet, Clever Species: How Unique Are We?* (2003), p. 215

The ultimate means of settling disputes

War has been defined as politics by other means. That is, war is a means of settling disputes. As long as there is a finite amount of something that people want, as long as desire exceeds the objects of desire, there will be disputes. War is the ultimate means of settling such disputes.

Limited resources

It all goes back to finite resources. There was the rich valley of milk and honey. It could support a certain number of people. Or put it another way, there were tribes all over the land but there were only a few beautiful, bountiful valleys. Who should have the valley, tribe x, y or z? Well, tribe x was there first. That ought to settle it.

But the leader of tribe y said, so what? Why should those losers get all the milk and honey? What about us? Aren't we deserving? And besides, tribe x has been there for years. It's only fair that we have a chance.

Or tribe z said, but we are smarter and prettier and therefore we deserve the rich valley. That is only right!

Tribe x said, we own the valley. It is ours. Tribe z said, property is theft!

And so they might argue on and on. Instead, tribe y just came in with stone axes flying and killed everybody in sight, except those that ran away and some women, and forcibly took over the valley. That settled it. Politics by other means.

After a while tribe x got its act together and came back and slaughtered all the (now) fat cats in the valley and regained the territory.

Rules into laws

And so it went. Humans could easily talk themselves into any kind of rationale for who deserves what, and what is fair, etc. So there had to be an arbitrator, a referee if you will, who could not be contradicted and whose rule always prevailed. That would be war. Dead men not only tell no tales, they drink no milk and they eat no honey, and they have no desires. End the other guy's desires and your desires will prevail.

The war system then worked. It became universal. If you want something enough to kill and risk being killed for it, then, hey, it can be yours! (But prove it.)

Humans are expendable. So much protoplasm running about can easily be recycled.

But it is not entirely comfortable in the valley when one realizes that not only will a new tribe be coming over the hill soon or late with battle axes held high, but even the guy in the grass shack next door may feel that he wants your spot in the valley and take it, forcibly.

In other words, the war system reduced to its most elemental parts (individual warriors) was the war of all against all. There was no security. All that was won today could be lost tomorrow. If I am free to kill you, you are free to kill me. Furthermore, humans are social beings and they need friends.

So within the tribe certain rules developed—laws. No killing other tribal members. No stealing their goats and no hanky-panky with the other guy's wife, etc.

Now a little security and bliss could descend over the inhabitants of the valley—at least until the barbarian hordes from the north came over the hill.

The law of the jungle

There was some attempt to apply the rules to the barbarian hordes, but they could not see how their security and their ability to pursue happiness was enhanced by following these rules as long as they were living among barren rocks while the rule makers were in the land of milk and honey.

So they applied the law of the jungle and attacked.

And so it went, and so it goes.

As of this date in human history, the year, say 50,001 (since we became behaviorally modern humans) the problem of limited resources in the face of unlimited desire has not been solved.

Except through the war system.

The war system works, albeit at a price.

Since it works, it will not be abandoned until something better comes along.

A substitute for war?

When I was young I liked to think that someday people would just agree to play a game to resolve the irresolvable and abide by the decision. A boxing match. A chess match. Or some other test of skill. However, this would not really resolve the issue. The two sides might agree beforehand to accept the result. However, the issue might be so important that for the side that lost, it would be intolerable and they would resort to some other means of getting what they want. What means is that? Ultimately the intention is to put the other side in a position in which they cannot do anything to change the result. Usually this means to kill them or drive them away, enslave them. Such results are actually the only results that really work regardless of the issue. That is why war is unlikely to go away anytime soon.

Ultimately, in the very long run it may go away, but that will only happen with world government and the universal rule of law. Even in such a society there will be those who are dissatisfied with their lot and will use violence in an attempt to achieve their ends. This will not be "war" per se. It will be criminal activity, and it will be handled by the criminal justice arm of the society.

Another bugaboo in the idea of the elimination of war is that without this ultimate test humans may become degenerate. This is what war lovers and people like Nietzsche believe.

For most of my life I have seen war as a terrible waste, as the ultimate stupidity, as a kind of madness. However when I recall H. G. Wells's passive Eloi and the aggressive Morlocks who ate them, I see something else. When I imagine the end of war and the end of aggression and the end of our willingness to murder and destroy, I realize that should we lose all that, we would become something like the Eloi and would go the way of the dodo, almost literally.

But who would kill us? War is only necessary when there are unfulfilled desires or threats to our security. Imagine a planet without any aggression, where everybody lived in peace and harmony, where the Golden Rule always applied, where no one harmed another.

I see a wolf

What I see when I tried to imagine such a place is a cow. No one eats this cow obviously. I see a wolf. Well, the wolf eats the cow. I see us eating proteins and carbs and fats derived from great vats of microorganisms. The wolf does not live by the Golden Rule. Eventually the wolf evolves enough smarts to eat the humans without getting caught. There are no diseases because we killed off or somehow protected ourselves from the bacteria and parasites that would eat us. Viruses we have killed or made innocuous.

But then I see a larger picture. We have killed or otherwise changed all our enemies, including ourselves, so that they no longer exist or can harm us. We have changed ourselves. But this is just a temporary place, a stop gap time before the wolves evolve, before the bacteria evolve, before the beings from outer space invade, before the nearby supernova blows...

We live on a darkling plane where ignorant armies clash by night (Matthew Arnold). We live on the plane of food, where every living thing is both the eater and the eaten (the Upanishads).

But what about plants? They eat only the sunlight and the air, water, and some minerals from the earth. Can we not be like the plants?

Yes, and seemingly better from a moral point of view. However the plants are not so innocent. Unchecked they crowd out the other plants. They take their water. The strangler vine grows up and around the tree slowly increasing its grip until the tree dies. The magnolia tree covers the ground with it leaves so that nothing else can grow. Some plants deposit poisons in the ground to keep other plants from growing. A great plain of tall grasses may eventually give way to the climax forest in which all living things constantly struggle to live and reproduce.

Conflict is inevitable '

The bottom line is simply that the mechanism of reproduction, of replication driven by the purposeless, mindless force of evolution leads inevitably to conflict and the resolution of conflict to more conflict to resolution to stasis—always temporary, always in flux, always waiting for the next great or small climate change or the next large meteorite or Ort Cloud disruption, the next turn round the galaxy, the next supernova.

And then change. Always, forever change.

And to what purpose?

A television commercial shows a girl new to the high school trying to find a seat in the cafeteria. She sits down with a group of girls who immediately all get up and leave. As a male my feeling, if I was the new girl, would be to take one of those girls and just beat the shit out of her. But for the girl that wouldn't solve her problem because if she was able to beat up one of the girls she would just invite retaliation or be just that much more ostracized. This is a key difference between men and women, and why, if we want to get beyond the war system, we have to have more women leaders.

An end to war?

War may end someday. We might have a planet with a world-wide government. The rule of law may prevail. This day will precede the day when there is no longer any crime. But when that happens we will no longer be humans as we are now. Humans kill one another if the need is great enough—if they perceive that the need is great enough. Humans are wonderful when they have enough to eat, when they are healthy, when they are confident and have dignity. But should any of these things be missing, they will try to gain them. Ultimately they will do anything that works, and they will form in their mind rationalizations to justify what works, whatever it might be.

I was surprised to learn recently that many soldiers in combat will not actually pull the trigger, and those that do will often aim high. But jihad warriors or kamikaze pilots are able to kill because they believe they are killing in the name of a higher power, and that is what the shaman and priests of old did for a living—got the young men to kill. Killing members of your own tribe is even much harder to do. In fact it's a taboo. The way to get humans to kill humans is to somehow make it clear that the others are *not* human, that they are cockroaches, subhuman, vile creatures, etc. That way the taboo learned from birth is circumvented.

Chapter Six:

Politics

Class politics

Plato wanted wise philosophers to rule. The problem with wise philosophers is that however wise they may be they will still rule in such a way as to benefit themselves, their families, friends, and their class. Of course if Plato were alive today he would probably expand "wise philosophers" to include the extended educated class since those wise in philosophy today would be expert in far too narrow a field. So perhaps we might say that the Platonic ideal today would be for the best educated and most experienced and, yes, the wisest men and women to rule.

The first problem with that is to realize that the best educated would be people who had the opportunity to become the best educated. They would be the privileged. They would want to maintain their privileged position. In some cases this might involve going against their own city, state or country. In fact what has sometimes happened historically is that one country's ruling class and its older males have declared war on another country with the idea of helping that country's ruling class. One of the main (hidden) objectives was to kill off a perceived excess of young males not of the ruling class in both countries.

War is politics by other means and this is an example of class politics across borders.

Two Cheers for Democracy

Democracy was always a bit suspect, mainly, I thought, because it wasn't pure, and couldn't be made pure. In a modern society the average person, who has to make a living and take care of the family, really doesn't have time to become fully informed about all the issues that might arise. Consequently, representative democracy, in which we vote for people to represent our point of view, was necessary. Direct democracy in which each person directly votes on every issue was clearly out of the question.

This is problem number one because our representatives end up voting for what the majority of their constituents want or what they themselves want. On the one hand, this is good because voting for what the majority want is really just an extension of direct democracy. And occasionally voting their own beliefs might be seen as a form of leadership. (At least that's what politicians are apt to claim.) However sometimes the representatives would vote for whoever gave them the most money. In fact this happened a lot and was a big problem. Still such people were sometimes found out and thrown out of office and the system managed to work—more or less. Witness the United States throughout much of its history.

Then came modern media and the ability to influence vast numbers of not fully informed citizens. Oh, boy. And add to that the fact that access to that media could only be reliably had through lucre, and one begins to the see the modern problem. Those with the cash could have a disproportionate effect on elections. Given the two party system in which only one of two candidates can (realistically speaking) attain high office, it is easy to see that those with the money might be able to pre-select candidates for both parties and thereby assure that somebody representing their interests would be elected. Note that big corporations typically give to the candidates from both parties. They can't lose.

> *Money Party, n.: The monolithic political party rumored to govern the United States. Said to camouflage its monopoly on power by periodically hiring new actors to serve as presidents, senators, and congressmen.*
> —Alex Boese, *Hippo Eats Dwarf: A Field Guide to Hoaxes and Other B.S.* (2006), p. 241.

At bottom the problem is human nature, human stupidity, the human propensity to be led, to be propagandized, to be influenced by media, the charismatic leader, and the herd mentality. In other words, depending on the masses to elect good leaders is like depending on the average guy to perform brain surgery.

So the founding fathers and indeed the people who managed to form or change governments worldwide sought to put some brake on the whims of the herd. In the U.S. this is called checks and balances, a "republican" form of government in which the will of the majority is restrained to some very real degree. Some things are left to the states and some to the federal government. There is a Constitution which says that popularly elected leaders cannot do certain things. There is a legal system that can try popularly elected leaders who break the law. This means that the leaders need to change the Constitution in order to get around it—which slows down the rampaging herd.

Furthermore, the judges are appointed for life and tend to be old fogies who tend to be conservative and likely to be opposed to any abrupt change from the rabble. And of course there is a House of Representatives whose members are up for election every two years, who en masse have the ability to block the desires of a president gone amuck. And just in case these johnny come lately representatives are too gung ho, there is a Senate composed of people elected once every six years, a body in which the lawmakers from the least populated state in the union have the same power as those from the most populated. Now THAT ought to put a damper on the rampage of the hoi polloi!

So a pure democracy is just an ideal that the powers that be would never tolerate.

I used to think this was a shame. But now that I have grown older and seen human nature in the raw for lo these many years (and even looked into my own heart) I can say "two cheers for democracy" and be very thankful that there are brakes on the will of the populace. After all Hitler was democratically elected. Plato was not far off when he postulated that wise philosophers ought to rule. However aside from the fact that they would tend to put the interests of their class first, there was no way (no authority) to separate the wise philosopher from the fake or corrupt philosopher.

The shallow men

The U.S. system then of a republic and other systems in Europe and elsewhere in which the will of the majority is watered down and checked to some extent has proved workable and perhaps best. However, what has happened in the U.S. during the last half century or so has resulted in the most incredible progression of mediocre and morally corrupt politicians without a real "statesman" in sight. From Lyndon Baines Johnson through Nixon and Reagan and Clinton and then the worst of them all George W. Bush, we have had some of the sorriest excuses for leaders in the history of the world (at least for a large state). (The jury is still out on Obama.) Where are the Washingtons and the Lincolns? The reason we get these mediocre and shallow men is because of the way the system works. The power brokers who control the media and access to it only allow candidates that will maintain their interests to be candidates. These tend to be men who have no values other than a lust for power, men who will sell out to the highest bidder, men whose main talent is getting elected.

But enough about the failings of representative democracy in 21st century America. Clearly we are now a decadent society. Like all decadent societies we will be overthrown or conquered soon or late. Indeed, it is necessary that the rascals be thrown out periodically because they inevitably become corrupt. If the system itself does not allow for that—and all the power within the system works hard against its being thrown out—then eventually there will come the revolution. It is not pleasant (for this American at least) to contemplate an end to America as we know it; however all empires fall eventually.

I mention all this as a way of saying that I no longer believe in democracy. I think there must be a better system. However, it may be that I no longer believe in human beings since there may be no better system than democracy. Alas.

Left vs. Right; liberal vs. conservative

You might have read somewhere (e.g., Wikipedia, which has a long discussion) that the origin of the terms left and right as applied to political persuasions comes from the way the French Assembly was seated in chamber circa 1791. The conservatives or royalists sat on the right and the liberals or revolutionaries sat on the left. Feuillants vs. Montagnards

There are two things wrong with this. First, the question is right or left from which point of view, that of the assembled or that of those addressing the assembly? I'm sure this has been established. My point is how little it matters which side was which, as long as conservatives are considered right wing and liberals left wing. Second, the association of "right" as in the right hand with a conservative point of view or philosophy and the association of "left" with the left hand and a point of view in opposition to the status quo goes back many, many centuries before there was a French Assembly.

This is easy to see without any recourse to history. What is "right" is more likely to be what is, has been, and continues to be, which is a conservative orientation. What is not right, that is, what is in opposition to the conservative orientation is left. Our word "sinister" comes from the Italian word for left. The vast majority of people are right-handed, something over 85 percent. This coincides with the simplistic idea that being conservative is "right" or correct and being in opposition to it is left or "sinister" or incorrect.

Two things to notice here. One, the present order is always right, and it is always wrong at the same time. What was liberal during the 18th century is now considered conservative. Most people during most times support a conservative agenda. They have grown accustomed to the way things are. They have adapted. Any change is therefore looked upon with suspicion at the very least and with dread and fear at the very most. Those out of power with little to lose in terms of property tend toward the left. Those in power are almost certainly on the right.

Furthermore, young people tend to be more left than older people. This only makes sense because the older people have more property and other goodies while young people have less.

The real question is which orientation is it better to follow, and the answer of course is, it depends. It depends on who you are, what your position and station in life is; and it also depends on the current state of affairs, politically, economically and otherwise.

Most periods in human history are periods in which it is better to go along with and adjust to the status quo than to take arms against it and risk life and limb. However every once in a while (and inevitably over the long run) things get so corrupt, so inbred, so unfair that a large number of people are willing to risk life and limb to get a larger piece of the pie. These times are times of revolution and are greatly feared by the powers that be. In the United States the political structure anticipates the revolution and so far has thrown the rascals out before they were in power too long.

Change is inevitable

There is a curious phenomenon that develops over time. The world changes and it almost always changes in the direction of those who are dissatisfied with the status quo. Part of this phenomenon is in the very nature of change itself. The conservatives do not want change: therefore they can seldom be the instruments of change. Since change is inevitable it is always the case that what is is always under fire and inevitably will change in some way.

What people really want is stability. They want the changes to take place in an orderly, measured fashion so that they are able to adjust to the changes as they take place, and there is little pain. Change almost always means pain for somebody.

It is my belief (and I'll bet that neuroscience will eventually support this view, if it hasn't already) that a conservative orientation is instinctive, or to state it another way, is built into the genes of a certain significant percentage of the population. I also believe that some people (clearly a minority) have genes that dispose them toward a liberal or a change-friendly point of view. And then there are people who are disposed genetically in neither direction, but adopt their views based on their experiences in life and on their circumstances. I would guess that it breaks down this way: 45% born conservatives; 40% born with no bias and 15% born with a liberal bias. Just a guess.

From an evolutionary point of view this would seem to be broadly correct. Most creatures that exist are adequately adapted to their environments. However their environments are constantly changing. Therefore at some point they may *not* be adequately adapted to their environments unless they change. So for the entire species to continue to simultaneously be adapted and yet ready to change there would need to be genes for both maintaining the status quo and some genes that work toward changing with the changing environment; and furthermore a kind of mechanism that would allow the expression of change to come to the fore when it needs to; that is, when the times they are a-changing fast, which sometimes happens. When a change is needed the body politic would then add the not-genetically-biased types to the dyed in the wool liberals to achieve a temporary majority. We have seen this happen historically many times. The numbers need not be exact of course. Sometimes a revolution can come about from a very aggressive minority. However for any revolution to succeed there must be a significant portion of the population dissatisfied with their lives.

They say you get more conservative as you get older. You usually have more to conserve for one thing. For another you have grown accustomed to the way things are. Change grows more inconvenient as we age.

Taxes and the conservative agenda

Taxes are what you pay to keep the warlords at bay. Governments can only exist through taxation. That's how they get paid. The problem with taxes is purely political. Politics is about who gets what, when, where and how. The government can rob you just as the warlord can, and if citizens are not vigilant they will indeed get robbed, and even if they are vigilant they will still get robbed, although perhaps not as much.

You often hear the rhetoric from the right intoning: "You earned it. You ought to be able to keep it!" But this simplistic slogan ignores the fact that even the road you drive on was built and paid for by somebody else. All the riches that can be created today out of the economy cannot be considered riches that you or I earned alone. Without the vast infrastructure already in place we would be as poor as African Bushmen. And yes the rich should pay more in taxes since they have more to conserve and protect, and therefore benefit disproportionately from the military, the police, and all the other institutions of government aimed at insuring domestic tranquility and safety—and that includes social welfare services which help keep the masses from the ramparts.

Taxes are the price we pay to live with relative security in a civilized world. Republicans know this, and they realize their job (usually their most important or only political job) is to keep taxes as low as possible. Shrink government. Democrats see taxes as a way of redistributing wealth, a way of leveling the playing field, a way of taking away some of the advantage the rich and powerful have. Taxes are the prime material of the give and take, the push and pull of the political process. As long as we have government we will have taxes. And if you don't like that consider the alternative. The alternative is anarchy which always dissolves into rule by the strongest and most violent.

Government is a necessary evil, one might say (in fact Hobbes did say). Republicans say this. Democrats believe that government can be used for good, that government can be an instrument for improving the lot of people. Both Republicans and Democrats are right, and both are wrong.

Rethuglicans

When Republicans talk about "family values" what they mean is ensuring paternity and institutionalizing sex. A Rethuglican is like a crocodile. It doesn't need to get smarter. It is close to its reptilian brain. It has survived since the time of the dinosaurs by being very good at subsistence and reproduction. It does what is necessary to eat and reproduce. Anything else is extraneous and suspect.

Republicans believe in killing their enemies. And they believe they will always have enemies. They believe that in matters as important as sex, war, or elections to positions of power, etc., one does what is necessary to win. Period. Anything else is naïve. They listen closely to their most primitive emotions and they follow their feelings instinctively. Gay marriage and homosexual sex disgusts them (as they once believed that mingling the races disgusted them). So it's wrong. They believe in using the environment for their purposes, and the environment includes other people. The great unwashed masses are to be used—kindly if possible, but used nonetheless—and if necessary to be enslaved or otherwise dominated economically and politically. This is just common sense to a Republican. They believe if the shoe is on the other foot, that foot will be kicking you in the face. They have a very cynical attitude toward humans because they have looked into their own souls.

In truth they are not completely wrong. But as somebody (actually Katharine Hepburn in the movie, *The African Queen*) once said, "human nature is what we are put on this earth to rise above." Not that I personally believe this, but I do believe that it is a good thing to aspire to something greater than our animal nature. Republicans believe that such notions are starry-eyed pap for the masses to be presented in TV commercials for propaganda purposes, the way ExxonMobil and the coal companies put cute little girls, green fields and flowers in their ads.

Bleeding heart liberals

Democrats believe that people are essentially good, and if not, they can be molded into goodness.

Democrats believe in pie in the sky and a free lunch, free sex, free love, free speech and a Dionysian festival once a month. They are touchie-feelie and love to wallow among the human masses especially at Grateful Dead concerts. They believe the goal of life is to wake up in the morning with a hard-on, roll over and love the one you're with, and then go back to sleep until time for the free lunch.

Dems believe in substance use not abuse. They believe we live in the best of all possible worlds except for greedy CEOs and right wing sickies and other anal-types in Human Resources.

Bleeding heart liberals believe that if you're nice to child molesters and serial killers they'll be nice to you. Dems believe if you coddle criminals and hold them to your warm breast they will see the error of their ways and go back to school to study sociology with a view to counseling the homeless on Sundays with the radical preacher from the Free Love Church.

Democrats tend to paranoia and believe in vast conspiracies. They know that aliens walk among us, and the government is covering up the truth about the face on Mars and what really happened at Roswell, as well as withholding the facts about who really killed Kennedy. They believe that ExxonMobil owns a patent to an internal combustion engine that gets 100 miles per gallon and runs on water.

Democrats have "issues." They believe they're fat for a reason and that reason has nothing to do with what or how much they eat. It's because Big Agriculture is force feeding them and Big Pharma has poisoned their water. They believe their kids are not in honors classes because they're "misunderstood" and discriminated against, and that the rich get richer and the poor get poorer because it's a vast right wing conspiracy.

Democrats believe in working for the man as long as they get 20 sick days a year, a month for vacation and two weeks for "issues" counseling, and membership in a grievance committee that meets once a month with full pay and time and a half.

Right and wrong

To elaborate with perhaps not as much satire, I would say that you can tell if you are inclined toward the Republican or right wing side of the aisle if you believe strongly in following your sense of disgust, of fear, of what you believe is morally right in making decisions—in other words, if you base your sense of right and wrong primarily on your sense of disgust and xenophobia.

You are more likely to be a Democrat if you believe that humans can figure out on their own without reference to instinctive feelings what is right or wrong, and they can do that based on evidence or by reasoning out the situation.

If you believe that a certain percentage of the human race just wants to lie around and do nothing productive, then you are a Republican. If you think that is a good thing you might be a Democrat.

Conservatives without conscience?

...[C]onservatism is a partially heritable personality trait that predisposes some people to be cognitively inflexible, fond of hierarchy, and inordinately afraid of uncertainty, change, and death. People vote Republican because Republicans offer "moral clarity"—a simple vision of good and evil that activates deep seated fears in much of the electorate. Democrats, in contrast, appeal to reason with their long-winded explorations of policy options for a complex world.

—from WHAT MAKES PEOPLE VOTE REPUBLICAN? [9.9.08] by Jonathan Haidt as found on the Website "Edge"

Within the 40% of the population that are reliably conservative there is a hardcore center that I like to call "congenital conservatives." Political psychologist Bob Altemeyer identified them as "authoritarian conservatives." John Dean in his book, *Conservatives without Conscience* (2006) quotes Altemeyer as saying, "Probably about 20 to 25 percent of the adult American population is so right-wing authoritarian, so scared, so self-righteous, so ill-informed, and so dogmatic that nothing you can say or do will change their minds." (p. 184) These are the same kind of people who supported Hitler's rise to power and voted for George W. Bush. They support authority and whoever is in power along with opposing change in every society in the world, and they have done that since well into the prehistory.

For what it's worth, John Dean puts "conservatives without conscience" into two main camps, (1) the leaders who orientate toward "social dominance," and (2) their followers, "right-wing authoritarians." If a person scores high on both "social dominance orientation" and "right-wing authoritarianism," that person is said to be a "Double High authoritarian." Examples of Double High authoritarians include the people whose photographed faces appear across the cover of Dean's book. They are: I. Lewis "Scooter" Libby, Vice President Dick Cheney's former chief of staff; Tom Delay, disgraced former Senate Majority Leader from Texas; Jack Abramoff, indicted lobbyist; Dick Cheney (intrepid hunter of caged birds thrown in the air); Karl Rove, mastermind of the seduction of Christian evangelicals; Bill Frist, M.D., Tennessee senator who once pretended to save cats from animal shelters only to cut their hearts out—literally, see Dean's book, p. 154; and Pat Robertson, evangelical Christian leader to whom God often speaks after doing some mischief in the world.

All of these people are Republicans and that is the major point that Dean is making. These guys and others like them have taken over the Republican Party, have sullied the name of conservatism, and are hell bent for leather to take over the country.

Dionysian liberals

Within the segment of society that is reliably liberal there is a hardcore center, perhaps five to seven percent of the population, who might be called Dionysian liberals, people who are socially tolerant, who always root for the underdog and identify with the counterculture while readily accepting change. They too are born that way.

The rest of the population may lean one way or the other or stay in the middle. Some may change from conservative to liberal but usually it's the other way around, liberal when young and conservative when older.

Then there are those who are "true believers," people who are always finding the one true religion. They tend to believe in something, regardless of the evidence, innately or based on some personal psychological experience usually of a dramatic nature. They can start out as communists and end up as skin heads.

The mentality of "us" versus "them"

It wasn't always this way. Before the rise of patriarchal, war-centered religions such as developed in the Middle East, we had fertility religions. This was before agriculture and animal husbandry when humans were essentially hunters and gatherers. In such societies the conservative-liberal-neither innate distribution was probably more like 33-33-33. The point is that once there were settled communities with storehouses of grain and other valuables, including large numbers of settled people who could be taken as slaves, the war system developed because there was a lot to be gained by waging war. This led to the follow-the-leader mentality and the rise of religious ideas that supported dying for the good of the tribe, the "chosen" tribe of God, etc. which ushered in a new kind of mentality that branded those who thought differently as traitors.

Conservatives don't just conserve, they have belief systems that are strongly "us" versus "them," that allow them to put a high premium on protecting "us" and killing "them." They tend to xenophobia and have the kind of mentality that sees only members of their race or tribe or state as fully human.

If the tribe becomes too conservative it loses the ability to change with changing circumstances and becomes less adaptive and may die out. It may too blindly follow stupid leaders leading to disaster (think George W. Bush for thirty years). Conservatism likes to crush creativity in any area except that of warfare (generally speaking) which is not always the best strategy evolutionarily speaking. Societies need liberals because there comes a time when things are so corrupt that change is really the best option.

End of an empire?

Ours was once a great country, arguably the greatest country in the history of the world. And all empires do indeed eventually turn to dust as does the flesh. Corruption is endemic and eventually it destroys. We began to lose our moral compass in the Cold War and with George W. Bush we even lost sight of the North Star. And yes, liberals need to get out their Machiavelli! And they need to take off the kid gloves and realize that because the right appeals to prejudice and limbic emotion, they are at a disadvantage. As it is said, "the conservative view requires no thinking." Most people in most cultures are conservative. It is the default position. And rightly so since we become adapted to the environment and so naturally want to keep things as they are. But when things change—and in the modern world, they change quickly— we must use more than the brain stem, we must use the neocortex. This is difficult for the conservative mind set.

Liberal-conservative, left-right, Democrats-Republicans are essential polarities of the political

71

makeup of humans. In essence the body politic maintains itself by this dialectic.

Chapter Seven:

Some Psychology

We have to learn to swim in the sea of the fish.

All God's children got animal talents.

Strength implies weakness; weakness implies strength.

High status in the tribe leads to reproductive success. This is why we are driven to flash our status like a mockingbird flashes its wings.

The difference between the old and the young is greater than the difference between humans and chimps.

We see what we want to see. We see what we expect to see.
One of the great delusions of the twentieth century science was to overrate nurture verse nature.

The "I" is a moving target

In certain situations humans are helpless to save themselves. Consider the case of the Hatfields and McCoys, the Palestinians and the Israelis, fishermen and their fish (the tragedy of the commons), whalers and their whales, humans and their reproductive capacity. And so on. Unless there is an outside agent, they will continue their present behavior until catastrophe.

The mind and the "self" are continually being created and maintained through interactions among the neurons and the modules of the brain, the other systems of the body, and the environment. The ancient query "Who am I?" can only be answered in this way, namely with the realization that the "I" is a moving target, continually dying and continually being recreated while maintaining a semblance of what it was before and what it will be.

The mind is an epiphenomenon of biological evolution. Epiphytes are plants that grow on trees. Minds are phenomena that grow on the brains of organisms.

I learned everything I need to know from song lyrics. E.g., "Freedom's just another word for nothing left to lose," which means possessions tie you down. If you have a dog you're less free to travel. If you own a house you're less free to move since you would have to sell the house or rent it out and that's a hassle and you may lose money. Even other people can tie you down, friends, relatives, colleagues, your spouse.

We have six senses.

Emotions

Daniel Goleman's book *Emotional Intelligence* made quite a splash when it came out in 1995. However, the book's title is a bit misleading since the book is really about social intelligence. While it appears that Goleman is trying to make a case for changing emotions, what he really makes a case for is changing behavior. "Emotional intelligence" really means intelligence about emotions. We aren't going to change our emotions, but we can change how we behave relative to those emotions.

However I don't necessarily go along with the general idea that emotions, instruments of the evolutionary mechanism, can or should be much influenced by society except in self-defense. The purpose of many emotions is to drive the individual in a direction consistent with the needs of the species mechanism regardless of what society or the individual wants. The needs, concerns and prejudices of any given society are relatively ephemeral notions compared to the evolutionary imperative, and in many cases it's a good thing we have instincts that override what society wants.

An excellent book on the subject of emotions and feelings is *Looking for Spinoza: Joy, Sorrow, and the Feeling Brain* (2003) by Antonio Damasio. He makes the argument that feelings are *perceptions* of the state of the organism. The concomitant emotions drive our behavior.

We domesticate ourselves

It is believed by some that wild animals are smarter than the domesticated kinds; and this has led some to think that wild humans were smarter than today's domesticated kind. Peter Ward in his book *Future Evolution* (2001) quotes neurologist Terry Deacon as saying that "all domesticated animals appear to have undergone a loss of intelligence compared with their wild ancestors." To the extent that we domesticate ourselves, we are dumber than our hunter-gatherer ancestors.

Anyone who lives the life of a couch potato and a passive boob tube watcher is probably less intelligent than the average person and less intelligent that he or she once was. Slow the flow of blood to the brain and it doesn't work as well. A recent finding is that obese people have eight percent less brain tissue than normal-weight people. Their brains look sixteen years older than brains from lean individuals. This is from a study done by UCLA Professor of Neurology Paul Thompson. You can find the story on the Web at Live Science.

The hunter gatherer societies of today have been pushed into the most undesirable land. Ronald Wright in his book, *A Short History of Progress* (2004) claims that the bodies of people living in the first agricultural societies were stunted and there was more evidence of malnutrition compared to the bodies of the hunters and gatherers. We have recovered somewhat from that but may be undergoing a new degeneration due to cheap and easy food and lack of exercise.

We always had an enemy. Humans don't know how to live without an enemy. If at any time we should be without an enemy, we'd have to invent one.

Accidents happen

Almost everything we do is directed toward subsistence or reproduction. Almost. It is one of the paradoxes of life and a property of the evolutionary mechanism that there are some things we do that are not in accordance with subsistence or reproduction. Just as the copying mechanism of reproduction is, and must be, imperfect for evolution to work, so must our behavior be imperfect in order for us to have the flexibility to meet unusual circumstances.

So occasionally (very occasionally) someone somewhere may do something that is not directed toward sex or subsistence. It happens. Accidents also happen and people sometime do something that defies logic or necessity. I don't know whether to categorize these behaviors as accidental or random. If you're thinking of works of art or jokes, just remember pleasing one's fellow tribe members is adaptive, and therefore beautiful works of art or engaging works of entertainment can be done for both sex and subsistence.

Without accidents, mistakes, or random behaviors, evolution could not operate. If we never took a different way home how much we would miss! If we never made a mistake and did things always in the same way, how would we grow? Mutations are an essential part of the evolutionary process. Random or mistaken or accidental behaviors are essential to the evolutionary testing of individuals. If everybody did everything in the same way how could any change come about? Olives from the tree are inedible. But long, long ago somebody tied an olive-laden branch to a Mediterranean vessel perhaps for luck or perhaps to see if fish would eat the olives, and after some time discovered that the now salty olives were not only edible but very tasty indeed. (Actually this discovery probably took place without the aid of vessels: maybe the olives were washed up upon a beach.) Notice that people had to practice another "mistaken" behavior for this discovery to take place, which was to taste the olives after their sea voyage!

If we were perfect biological machines we would always act in accordance with our self-interest except when that conflicted with the interests of the evolutionary mechanism.

Sometimes we must fool ourselves

What really is alive is the planet; what really has intelligence is the planet. All life is part of a web. The question is, are we the planet's brain—or its cancer? Are we in the process of becoming or just a dead end on the way to becoming? Will we become stewards of the planet or just the exploiters that our animal selves have naturally and—when our numbers were small—correctly been?

It is important to note that sometimes even a bad plan is better than no plan at all. If the man feels that he doesn't know where to start, that he has no clue about how to proceed, he might well give up before he begins. But give him a plan, an idea, that might even be wrong, and have him believe it, then he might proceed with some confidence.

This all goes back to "the man must fool himself." This is a basic fact of human existence. Sometimes things are so bleak that it is better that we not know the truth. Sometimes we are so guilty and so culpable that it is better that we lie to ourselves and proclaim in our heart of hearts that we are good and we did the right thing and all will be well. The storms rage about us, but we know that these storms are caused by the evil doing of the shaman, but we have a remedy. We say abracadabra three times forward and three times backward and the storms will subside. And in some cases, after a day or two, they do subside. We remember those times and misremember the times when the storm did not stop. Perhaps we miss-pronounced the abracadabra or maybe our heart wasn't sufficiently in our expression.

We pretend to know

Note how the belief in prayer or in doing God's will and the like can help the individual. Ironically, false beliefs may be adaptive. This is why conservative religious people insist on their lies and hypocrisy and why they overlook and condone the lies and hypocrisy of their leaders. We all see the lies and hypocrisy of politicians, shaman and other religious figures and wonder how the faithful can follow them. But for the faithful not to follow them is worse. Instinctively (and unconsciously) they know the lies are necessary. Consciously of course they haven't a clue, and don't want one. Following the leader even if he is wrong is better than going your own way. Cohesion of the tribe demands that you follow the leader wherever he may lead, especially in times of peril. The old saying, "my country, may she always be right, but my country right or wrong" sums it up.

This phenomenon exists because humans are limited creatures in a world we do not and cannot fully understand. The great trick of the evolutionary mechanism is to have humans combat this state of ignorance and powerlessness by simply pretending—but pretending in such a way that we do not know we are pretending. Remember the man who is lying may have some difficulty hiding his lie, but if he thinks he is not lying, how much easier it is for him to convince others of the truth of what he is saying.

When we do have the answer, when there is a truth we can find, when there is a plan that will work, then it is better of course to have the truth and to follow it instead of doing nothing or doing the wrong thing.

Weakness implies strength

In the sea of the fish the big fish eat the little fish. In the sea of human existence it is the same. Big in human terms does not necessarily mean big in size, although that is often the case. But because the human sea is a sea of intricate and dazzling complexity, a small fish may if he's careful and has certain talents avoid the big fish, and while he is healthy eat the smaller fish and make a fine living.

When you see a man who is small and ugly, unsophisticated, seemingly untalented and ignorant of all that is important, you are probably seeing some unlucky soul that when the gene machine spun out its latest lottery got a bunch of bad numbers. Maybe. But it is always wise to consider that with so much evolutionary "weakness" staring you in the face that he may have some talent that is not obvious, a talent that allows him and his kind to make a living in this world and reproduce.

A timid man may be considered careful. A dull person may have the ability to get by on very little. A stupid person may be strong of limb. An ugly woman may know where edible tubers are and how to scare the lions away. She may possess great love. In all the observations one might make about others, it is good and wise to realize that weakness implies strength, since if the person really is weak he or she wouldn't be here—that is, their type would have died out long ago.

Conversely, strength implies weakness. When somebody is beautiful of face and limb he or she has a great advantage sexually speaking. Such an advantage may compensate for weakness in other areas of life, such as gathering food or tracking animals.

People with great social skills and charisma are able to get others to do what they want them to do. There is perhaps no greater subsistence skill than the ability to get people to do what you want them to do. Heads of great corporations are typically not only smart, but charming and skillful at manipulating others.

Chapter Eight:

Consciousness

Our consciousness "is most likely just some vague foreshadowing of what would be called true consciousness..."

—David Grinspoon, *Lonely Planets: The Natural Philosophy of Alien Life* (2003), p. 396

Impenetrable literature

If I were to give awards for impenetrable literature I would award third place to political and economic philosophers (think Marx and Veblen), second place to corporate lawyers, and the grand prize to anyone writing on consciousness, with a special award to philosophers writing on consciousness. Even the very articulate Daniel Dennett can be very annoying!

It might be asked, why am I writing a chapter on consciousness to be read by the general public? In one sense this seems right since my theme is "the world is not as we think it is." No doubt the reader can expect that I will attempt to show that consciousness isn't what we think it is (and I will attempt to do that). But in another sense the topic of consciousness is so obtuse and so riddled with contradictory opinions by so many experts that it would seem a hopeless task to make sense of it. Furthermore, it seems such a heavy topic that the reader's eyelids must of necessity droop and perhaps close.

Consciousness defined

First let me quickly give my definition of consciousness as the term is generally used. It has three aspects:

One: awareness of the world (including awareness of our self and our processes, that is, self-awareness).

Two: self-identity. Notice that awareness of self is different from this *identification with* self.

Three: experience or sensation, the feelings we get when we experience the world. This is sometimes called "phenomenal consciousness." An example would be the subjective experience of the color red, or the taste of a strawberry.

The first aspect of consciousness, awareness, including self-awareness, is something that all (or nearly all) living things have. The range of awareness of course is large. A bacterium has awareness of the texture or feel of certain surfaces, an awareness of the molecules of certain substances in the air and perhaps heat as opposed to cold, and so on. It has a sense of self and not self to some primitive extent—I presume since it doesn't eat itself. Actually a bacterium is powerfully aware compared to a rock.

A primate has an awareness of so much that I won't attempt to reiterate.

The second aspect of consciousness, self-identity, is the subject of next chapter.

The third aspect of consciousness, feelings or sensation, is what is most mysterious (and trivial, by the way, compared to the other two) and is what has had philosophers in a tizzy since time immemorial. Quite simply there is no way that such subjective experiences can ever become objective. The experience of the red that I see may or may not be the same as the experience you have; and there is no way that we can say for sure whether our experiences are the same or different.

It would be useful if all writers on consciousness defined just which aspect of consciousness they are talking about. Without clear definitions we are speaking in babblese like postmodern theorists or corporate lawyers trying to obscure and muddle the true message. I am sorry to report that most writers on consciousness I have read fail to be clear about which aspect of consciousness they are talking about. I am willing to bet that sometime in the future people will look back and wonder what the gobbledygook was all about. I am somehow reminded of the medieval preoccupation of clerics with the problem of how many angels could dance on the head of a pin.

Consciousness is dynamic

John McCrone in his book *Going Inside: A Tour Round a Single Moment of Consciousness* (2001) sees the brain as a dynamic organism that creates its reality through a combination of sensory input and a constantly readied state of arousal that continually interprets the world and guesses about what to expect next, and then amends accordingly, again and again. Thus his point of view for examining how the brain works focuses on a "moment of consciousness."

McCrone makes the observation (p. 60) that "The idea of a bounded object [say, us] is really just a convenient fiction." Compare this with the quote from Einstein on page 31. McCrone recognizes that our brains and our minds are intimately connected to the world and cannot be understood alone. The brain is a dynamic entity, not only constantly changing, but constantly interacting with both the environment within and the environment without. Thus McCrone observes that "Given the real world is a continuous place, and so exact starting points can never be measured, this means that it is impossible—as a matter of principle—to predict the behavior of a feedback-dependent system [like the brain]" (pp. 64-65). (This is from chaos theory.) Ergo, the fall of a strict reductionism in the study of the brain and consciousness, and the ushering in of the realization that the brain must be understood in light of not only its composition, its components, and its developmental history, but its dynamic nature.

The brain predicts

Did you know that the way tennis players are able to react to a 140 mph serve is that they anticipate where the serve is going in part by reading the body language of the server before the ball is actually hit, and they don't even know they're doing it! In fact it is part of the brain's talent to predict. As it readies itself for the next moment, the brain makes a prediction of what that moment will be like. McCrone calls it "riding a wave of predictions" (p. 147).

The brain organizes itself as it grows in concert with the world. If you watch a baby closely, you can see that the baby is working very, very hard to make sense of its world.

Animal consciousness

In the penultimate chapter, "The Ape that Spoke," McCrone argues that the acquisition of language was critical to the development of consciousness. He states that "Animals are locked into the present tense," living "entirely in the here and now," and that "there is no reason to think that a monkey ever sits around mulling over the story of its life."

For those of us who have had close intimate relationships with animals, this is not so clear. Personally, I think animals such as cats and dogs do have some sense of self, and that they do have some experience of the past, and can anticipate the future to some degree. We really don't know about their level of self-awareness. We can be reasonably sure it is less than ours of course, but I think there is a tendency in some quarters to underestimate what animals know.

I also don't agree with McCrone's notion that "The invention of articulate, grammar-driven speech was also the invention of articulate, logic-driven thought" (p. 288). There was plenty of "logic-driven thought" before there was grammar; indeed animals often think logically, if their behavior is any indication. (And there is no reason to think it isn't, to echo McCrone's words above.)

I think that because some of us are such highly verbal people, we tend not to notice that we think and figure out things logically at a level deeper than that of language. Human language is often a translation of a more basic inner language. As above, I think it is important to make a distinction between "consciousness" meaning "awareness," and "consciousness" meaning "self-identity." Whenever the word "consciousness" is used, I cringe a little because I know it will mean different things to different people and there is the very real danger of talking past one another. Although McCrone does attempt to define consciousness as he goes along, he is to my mind not entirely successful. For example, on page 265 he writes, "So, again, what is consciousness? In some sense, it must be the outcome of a moment's processing." Perhaps—but what does *that* mean?

The half-second lag in our awareness

One of the things I learned in Tor Norretranders' *The User Illusion: Cutting Consciousness Down to Size* (1991, 1998) is that it takes half a second for our consciousness to be aware of what we're doing. We don't notice this time lag because the mind back-peddles and makes it appear that we are on sync. The mind must backtrack so that our system will know when in real time an event took place. Reactions to things like removing a hand from a hot stove occur faster than our consciousness has time to be aware is a good example. After something like that the mind just reconstructs the event and there is the illusion that we were aware in real time. We weren't.

Norretranders gives the example (p. 256) of a bicycle accident which happens too fast for the "I" to make a decision. The decision is made for the "I." So, is the "I" of consciousness really in charge or is that an illusion? The book's title, "The User Illusion" gives Norretranders's opinion. I tend to agree. This is similar to the Buddhist idea that the ego-I of consciousness is an illusion.

Norretranders makes a distinction between the "I" that is conscious and has a short bandwidth of perhaps 16 bits and the "Me" that is non-conscious and has a bandwidth of millions of bits. The "I" thinks it is in charge, but all it has is a slow-moving veto.

On pages 268-269 Norretranders talks about how to get Self 2 (corresponds to the Me) "to unfold its talents." One method is to overload the "I" so that the "Me" is allowed to come to the fore. Give the "I" "so many things to attend to that it no longer has time to worry" or "veto." Then the inner "Me" comes forward and plays beautiful music, etc. Similarly, we could say that the use of mantra, e.g., is effective as a meditation tool since it keeps the very verbal "I" occupied and allows the inner "Me" to come forward.

On the subject of the half-second delay in our conscious recognition of what is happening to us (discovered by Benjamin Libet, by the way) Norretranders writes: "If there were not half a second in which to synchronize the inputs, [from our senses] we might, as Libet puts it, experience a jitter in our perception of reality." (p 289)

Most of what we know can never be expressed

In reference to the title metaphor, we find on page 291: "The user illusion, then, is the picture the user has of the machine" [i.e., his body and brain] "...[I]t does not really matter whether this picture is accurate or complete, just as long as it is coherent and appropriate. It is better to have an incomplete, metaphorical picture of how the computer works than to have no picture at all."

On the 16-second bandwidth of consciousness: "The bandwidth of language is far lower than the bandwidth of sensation. Most of what we know about the world we can never tell each other."

Consciousness is restricting. It discards information from the environment and returns a distilled essence. We miss a lot because there is no evolutionary necessity that we be aware of everything our organism experiences. The vast amount of information would only confuse us, or at least make us less efficient. So consciousness is the veil of illusion that yoga, Buddhism, Hinduism, etc. talk about. Consciousness is *maya*.

A self-organizing ecosystem

We have to begin to think of the brain as a self-organizing ecosystem, one of such staggering complexity and delicate balance that almost any aspect of a patient's life may be relevant to a diagnosis or essential to treatment.

—John J. Ratey, from his book, *A User's Guide to the Brain: Perception, Attention, and the Four Theaters of the Brain* (2001), p. 354.

Consciousness as "an emergent property"

In James Trefil's book, *101 Things You Don't Know about Science and No One Else Does Either* (1996) he asks the question, "Will We Ever Understand Consciousness?" (pp. 15-17) His answer ("My own guess is that consciousness will turn out to be an emergent property of complex systems") is one that I would agree with substantially; but I wonder if Trefil really appreciates the implication of his answer when he hopes (against Francis Crick's view) that "human beings will be found to be something more than a 'vast assembly of nerve cells and their associated molecules.'" (p. 17) I wish he had speculated on what that "more" that might be. One senses that the mysterian in Trefil's soul is yearning to be out and about, but that Trefil's sense of (scientific) propriety is keeping him under lock and key.

In another book published the following year, *Are We Unique? A Scientist Explores the Unparalleled Intelligence of the Human Mind* (1997), Trefil argues that the difference between animal consciousness and human consciousness is more than just a difference of degree. He asserts that the difference is so great that it constitutes a difference of kind. When things get sufficiently complex we have the "emergent property" phenomenon from chaos theory. As others have said, more is different, and what emerges is something that cannot always be predicted.

"Deniers" and "mysterians"

Trefil surveyed the "landscape of opinion" on consciousness and came up with the following categories:

"Deniers," those who deny that there is a "problem of consciousness at all–that once you understand what the neurons are doing, there's nothing else to explain" (pp. 182-183). He puts Daniel Dennett in this category.

Next there are the "Mysterians," those who feel that the problem of consciousness will never be solved. And finally there are the "Materialists," like Francis Crick, who in his book, *The Astonishing Hypothesis: The Scientific Search for the Soul* (1994), asserts that we are "in fact no more than the behavior of a vast assembly of nerve cells and the associated molecules" as quoted above.

Trefil (who is a physicist) claims to be a member of this latter group. However I think that he has a lot of the "mysterian" in him. For example, he writes on page 173 that when he was courting his future wife he suddenly realized he loved her, and he realized he knew this with more certainty than he had ever known anything in physics or mathematics. He adds that an algorithm running on a Turing machine is never going to know anything in quite the same way.

I agree, but the knowing he is talking about is hardly just (or even) a knowing. It is a near total brain/body experience, and since he is an evolutionary, reproducing human being, it's a profound and extremely important experience. He isn't just "knowing." He is feeling and then some. Computers don't feel. So of course they cannot know something in quite the same way.

"Illusionists"

There are other (small) problems with Trefil's presentation, but I'll skip them and go straight to what I think is the most glaring: an omission of a category for those who believe that consciousness is simply an illusion, a device of the evolutionary mechanism. This category would include most evolutionary psychologists and Tor

Norretranders. From this point of view our consciousness is indeed an emergent property of the evolutionary process, a mechanism that forces us to identify with the particular phenotype that we are and to work tirelessly for its advantage and to fear its disadvantage, especially its death. A computer, which has not gone through the same sort of process, would not have a similar consciousness.

On pages 184-185 Trefil encounters this point of view from the "Illusionists," as I will call them, but misses the significance of what they said to him. He writes that the neuroscientists with whom he was talking were "apt to brush off questions about consciousness with a wave of the hand and, 'Oh, it's just an illusion,' then get back to their work." Trefils claims these people are "deniers," not realizing that there is a world of difference between calling something an illusion and saying it doesn't exist. Illusions exist, and can be very powerful. Our consciousness is an illusion we can't help but believe.

The birth of consciousness

I'd like to add that this idea of consciousness is an old one that can be found in the works of Buddhism, jnana yoga and the Vedas, and probably elsewhere. Our consciousness is an amazing experience, so overwhelming and so overpowering that it dominates all aspects of our existence. But it's just part of the illusion, the *maya* that separates us from the underlying truth of our existence. Our ego, our subjective sense of self, is also an illusion. Our individual consciousness is no different than the other person's. It is exactly the same: a mechanism of profound identification that fosters the delusion of separateness.

Metaphorically speaking, our consciousness is like the candle flame. It is essentially the same in every manifestation. What is "reborn" in Eastern religions is consciousness. However, reborn is not quite the right word.

The symbolic meaning of the Garden of Eden as a falling from grace is the standard model from non-literalist Christianity; however a broader view sees the Garden of Eden as the symbolic expression of the birth of human consciousness. Without consciousness we were "innocent" and then suddenly we saw that we were "naked." We became "conscious." We gained knowledge of good and evil, and we became aware of our animal nature.

Computer consciousness

I also want to point out that computers (or robots) will never become conscious in the same way that we are conscious. This fact and its explanation illustrate the fundamental difference between living things which evolve in concert with the environment and machines which are designed.

I was abruptly enlightened on the subject of a computer having consciousness when I stumbled onto the question of how one would program a computer to feel pain. When you really think about this problem it sheds light on the consciousness issue. The evolutionary system gave us pain so that we might not harm ourselves through carelessness. If we wanted a computer (call it the brain of a robot) to avoid doing harm to itself, we would program certain instructions into it. We would in effect prohibit it from hurting itself. A pain mechanism would not be necessary or—and this is really enlightening—possible. At least I haven't figured out how it might be done.

This helps to illustrate the difference between a machine and an organism, the first designed, the second evolved.

It might seem that if a computer becomes sufficiently complex it will, as in complexity theory, reach a critical state and then in a phase transition become conscious. I used to think, in some vague way, that this was inevitable. But there is an aspect of consciousness that cannot be programmed into a computer. A sufficiently intelligent and knowledgeable computer may know everything that is in all the libraries of the world, and would probably understand humans better than humans can understand themselves; it would certainly understand the dynamics of the world—ecologies, weather, etc., better than humans can, and so on. The consciousness of such a computer would include in our definition of consciousness, awareness, even self-awareness, but it would not have self-identity (except as programmed in) and most especially it would not have sensations or feelings, which is the mysterian aspect of consciousness.

You could program a computer to be aware of something touching it. We already do that when a computer is "touched" in certain places, such as on a screen, and we can say that the computer "feels" the touch and reacts to it. We have programmed the computer to react to the touch. We can even program a computer to react to being physically abused, such as having a knife stuck into it. But what we can't do is program a computer to feel pain. We can program the computer to act as if it feels pain. We can program it in theory to behave as though it feels pain, perhaps cry out, withdraw, take defensive actions, etc. But it will never feel pain.

It will not feel pleasure either. The upshot of all this is the realization that computer intelligence or computer consciousness is different than animal intelligence or animal consciousness.

As a thought experiment I recommend that you try to figure out a way to make a computer feel pain. As part of this experiment you might think about how animals develop the "ability" to feel pain. What came first the recognition that something was painful, or the sense of pain, or the sense that pain is painful? Did they evolve more or less simultaneously?

This is not to say that a computer can't become more aware than a human being or that a computer can't become "smarter" or more intelligent. It depends on how you define the words "aware," "smart" or "intelligent." Clearly it can become more aware in the normal sense of sensing and comprehending its environment.

Behavior is the real "emergent property"

Finally I want to put a finer point on consciousness so that we realize that consciousness is not an emergent property of the brain but is our subjective experience of an emergent property. It is a *perception*. Incidentally, this is why it is believed in Hinduism, for example, that our brains constitute a sixth sense, a way of perceiving the world in addition to the senses of taste, smell, touch, hearing and sight, and are *not*, e.g., calculating machines. We can "see" things that other animals cannot.

Another way to look at this is to understand that pain and pleasure, boredom and exhilaration, and all the other emotional experiences of humans (and animals) are mechanisms that work to direct our behavior in adaptive directions. The real emergent phenomena are our behaviors. Thus inert matter organized by evolution leads to the building of rocket ships to transverse space and to the cultivation of varieties of apples and grains to nourish the organisms that design and build those machines. The "consciousnesses" and the "feelings" experienced are not to be confused with the actual drawing of the blueprints or the tightening of the lug nuts.

Chapter Nine:

Self-Identity: A Thought Experiment

Self-identity is the simplest of the three aspects of consciousness but perhaps the most powerful. It is also the most ethereal.

Being "teleported"

What self-identity is can be demonstrated with a thought experiment. Suppose we have the ability to reduce your body into its elemental aspect: x number of atoms of oxygen, x number of atoms of hydrogen, carbon, zinc, etc. And from these atoms construct a new "you." Or to put it another way, suppose we have the ability to *transport* you from one place to another by first reducing your body to its elements and then reconstructing them in another place (the kind of "teleporting" done in science fiction, similar to the "Beam me up, Scotty" phenomenon of Star Trek.)

You get up in the morning and you go to the lab where you are sent to the other side of the room to be teleported, in this case to a place just a few feet away. This is done is something like one ten-thousandth of a second—at any rate so fast that you have no conscious awareness of it happening. Not only are all of the atoms of your body broken down and reconstructed, but also the atoms of the trillions of microbes that live in and on your body. The teleporting takes place in a room with a nearly perfect circle. No part of the circle is different from any other part. You go in, you stand on a line (which is a circle within a circle) and presto! nothing seems to happen. Observers in a two-way mirror can see that you have moved from a near part of the circle to a most distant part across the room.

You go home and talk about your day at the office. You kiss your wife and tell her, "I was teleported, but it was so fast that I wasn't aware of it. Just another day at the office." You play with the dog and help your kids with their homework.

Just send the information

At some point the engineers of teleporting decide that it would be a waste of energy to send the elements of your body long distances, say to the moon, when all that is necessary is the information about how those elements should be arranged. All of those elements are present on the moon. So it is proposed that they test this by making available in the lab a ready and sufficient supply of all the elements in your body. Since there is an ancient law on the books prohibiting the cloning of human beings, it is decided that (as before) your body will be broken down, and then the new you constructed on the other side of the room from elements brought in. (Just to keep this thought experiment tidy, imagine that the elements are brought in during the one ten-thousandth of a second that it takes to break you down and build you up. This way there is no distracting pile of elements on the floor across the room as you arrive.)

You go into the lab and they perform the new teleporting experiment and it works fine. You notice no difference at all, and when you get home to tell the wife after giving her a peck on the cheek, "They say it was different, but I didn't notice any difference." You play with the dog and help your kids with their homework.

Two identical yous

Then one day at work a mistake is made. The original you is not broken down and presto! there are now two identical yous in the room on opposite sides of the circle.

Ooops! We have a problem.

The lawyers are called in and after they consult for many hours it is determined that, by law, one of the yous has to go. But which one? (I forgot to mention that the inner circle of the room is constantly rotating at a moderate pace.) The engineers were so astonished at their error in not breaking down the first you, that they were unable to say which you was closer to their observation window and therefore they have no way of determining which is the new you and which is the old.

The question arises: can they find out by asking you?

They confer. Meanwhile the two yous continue to rotate slowly around the room. The engineers come to the obvious conclusion that since the yous are identical they will have the same memories, they will recall the same experiences, they will have the same abilities, etc. They realize there is no question they can ask that will help them to determine which of the two yous has to go.

The two yous thinking identical thoughts

Now let's focus on one of the yous. You are thinking that you are tired of going around in circles and you are beginning to worry about what the engineers are thinking. Clearly there is across the room from you an identical you. You are aware of the law against cloning and you wonder what they are going to do about it. The you across from you is thinking the same thing.

After some time you are sent to one of the suites reserved for out of town big-wigs that the company has in its buildings and told to relax, take a shower, watch some TV. What would you like for lunch? Maybe a little wine with lunch, and then home after a long day.

Some hours later you arrive home, kiss the wife, etc. "Very interesting day at the office," you tell her. "Have you been drinking?" she asks. You explain. She asks, "But...but...what about the other you? And how can I be sure that this is the original you?"

You have thought this out and reply, "It doesn't matter. I'm me and I'm here and I'm happy about that!"

Meanwhile back at the company you are being told that you will have to start a new life without your family. Sorry. You will be given a good job in another part of the country. You are devastated. "This isn't fair," you say. "I know I am the real original me." They nod sympathetically.

Bring in the accountants

At the same time the company's lawyers are conferring again, this time with the accountants. The lawyers have come to the regrettable conclusion that as long as two yous exist they might be discovered and the company would have to pay a stiff fine for cloning humans. The accountants point out that the way the situation is being handled it is almost a certainty that the mistake will be discovered because the elements used to make the other you will be missing from the company's accounts.

After conferring with the CEO and other high ranking officials it is determined that those elements will have to be restored to their proper place in supply. You (at home) are told to take the next day off. You (at the company) are told to sleep over and report for work as usual.

The next day the two yous go into the circular room and are broken down, but on the other side of the room the other you's elements are transported randomly into a jar.

You go home and then report for work the following day. The engineers are all smiles. The CEO comes down to shake your hand and tell you what a fine job you have been doing and you get a raise in salary.

Another ooops!

At another company they are also working on teleporting. The setup is a little different but the science is basically the same. You come into work and are "teleported" to the other side of the room. Their room is not circular and it doesn't rotate. You always noticed that after being broken down and reassembled, you end up on the other side of the room. One day a bizarre thing happens. You are standing there as always and the pop! another you comes to life on the other side of the room!

Ooops! They forgot to break down the original.

But wait a minute. This time you know you are the original. You saw the other you pop into existence. Ah, but the other you says he had exactly the same experience. He was standing there and suddenly another you popped into existence.

But this time you've got him. Because the room is square, it is not revolving, and anyway you always stand on the side of the room near the observation window and the drinking fountain. That you is on the other side of the room where the oil painting of the company's founder is hung. Nobody can deny that. (You are thinking fast because you know about the law against human cloning and you know it is likely that one of the yous will have to go, and since you are the original, it is not going to be you!)

The engineers confer. They hold off on calling in the lawyers. "Damn, we got ourselves a doozie here." They wax philosophically. What is the difference between the two? they ask. Nothing. Well, except identity. You number one identifies with you number one, and you number two identifies with you number two. After some further consideration they decide that there really is a difference between the two yous brought about by their different locations in space. The second you knows he is the clone because he knows where the founder's oil painting is. And the original you knows this too.

This time a decision is made about which "you" to send home to his wife and kids and which one to recycle. There was a small problem, however. The second you tried to escape and had to be tackled by security...

A variation on the thought experiment

The transporting company has come up with a new commercial application. It is offering people the opportunity to have themselves sent to the future! The idea is to make a complete informational map of a person and store that info and then reconstitute YOU sometime after you die. Not only will you come back to life perfectly as your former self, you will come back to life at an age you choose now!

Okay, you store yourself as information and then after some years you die. Then you are reconstituted (so to speak) and brought back to life. The question is then is it the same you? And how do you feel about that?

The same in everyone

The point of this thought experiment should be obvious. But then again interpretations may differ! At any rate it is clear to me that this sense we have of being ourselves, of me being me, and you being you, is something we all share. I identify with myself strongly to the extent that I want nothing bad to happen to me and only good. You feel the same way about yourself. It is an identification built into the human organism by the process of evolution. It has adaptive value. This self-identity is an imperative of the evolutionary mechanism, and the most important thing to understand about it is that it is the same in everyone.

Chapter Ten:

The Paradox of Free Will

We have and do not have free will. Free will is a paradox. If you spend some time thinking about free will and reading what others who have thought long and hard about free will, it is difficult to escape the conclusion that free will cannot possibly exist.

First there is the problem of the actor; that is, the entity that is making a "free" decision. Who is that actor? When you strip away all that you think is you what do you have left? What you have left is what you have left of the onion when all the layers have been stripped away. There is no homunculus there.

Swarm intelligence in the brain

A combination of neurons within brain modules, acting as swarm intelligence, dictates our actions. Those brain modules are the product of the evolutionary process. There is no ghost in the machine of our brain making decisions. It is hard to even imagine free will without a kind of Cartesian dualism, without a ghostly entity left after the layers have been stripped away, leaving some otherworldly essence.

But the fact that we do not have free will should not be anything but freeing. You must perforce behave as though you had free will. If you play harder you will win the game. If you work hard and make good decisions and

101

practice a good lifestyle you will be successful. If you don't, you will not be successful. So you make good decisions and are moderate in your habits. Somebody says, who are you kidding? You couldn't help but act the way you do. Your success is not due to your free will choices. Instead it is due to your nature which made you make the good decisions you made. So be it! And if you fail, well that too was your nature. There was nothing you could do about it. Your genes coded for sloth and overindulgence. What could you do?

So if you are successful, take the credit. If not, blame your genes and the fates. Today, this very minute, you are either going to go to the office and get on the phone to clients or you are going to pop open a can of beer, zip open a bag of Fritos, kick back and watch reruns of "The Simpsons." Which is it? You decide. If you don't like the prospect of failure and see little solace to be had in blaming your genes, you will get to work. Otherwise not. In either case it's okay. If you are about to become one of life's losers, you can still buck up and get it done. Like the particle/wave indeterminacy of quantum mechanics you simultaneously have free will and do not have free will.

The necessary illusion

From a societal point of view of course people have free will. From a legal point of view we have free will.

Benjamin Libet in *Neurophysiology of Consciousness: Selected Papers and New Essays* (1993) showed (as noted in the previous chapter) that when people make a conscious decision to do something, such as lift a finger in an experiment, they do so half a second after the neural activity correlated with the willing takes place. This would seem to argue against free will. In a sense there is in the organism a very ghostly presence that is composed of brain neurons and modules that is operating on our behalf independently of our conscious awareness. We have the illusion that we are making decisions, and this ghostly presence allows us to live happily in our ignorance. The illusion of being in charge is part of what consciousness is all about.

David N. Stamos in his book *Evolution and the Big Questions* (2008) asks what does consciousness do? How is it adaptive? If it gives us the illusion of being in charge, perhaps that in itself is adaptive. Someone who feels he has no say in something, who feels his efforts have no importance, who feels he is at the mercy of things he can't control may not be as effective in dealing with the environment as the man who feels that he is in charge— even if that feeling is an illusion.

We have the illusion that we are making decisions, and we live happily in our ignorance. To repeat: the illusion of being in charge is part of what consciousness is all about.

Hume's Fork: Either our actions are determined, in which case we are not responsible for them, or they are the result of random events, in which case we are not responsible for them.

There is no free will but there is contingency. You may through happenstance, or what seems to be a volitional choice, or through help from family or friends, etc. make decisions that result in giving you a better life than you would otherwise have had. You may read a book, meet a person, take a trip, etc. that will change your life for the better. There is the "you" of contingency, the you who did this and the you who did that. One might lead a better and more fulfilled life than the other.

Compatibilism

On free will in his book *The World's 20 Greatest Unsolved Problem*s (2005) John Vacca uses basically three authorities, Timothy O'Connor, Miroslav Backonja, and Paul J. Bertics, and from them constructs what he sees as the current understanding by neuroscience. I wasn't even aware that neuroscientists had a position on free will. I thought it was a purely philosophic or religious question. The opposing camps of naturalism (no such thing as free will) and libertarians (humans have free will) are reconciled in the neuroscientific community through the idea of "compatibilism." What it means is that the lack of free will (which most neuroscientists, Buddhists and myself, among others see as obvious) is made compatible with the societal and human psychological need to believe in free will (for punishment and criminal deterrence) by realizing that in an Orwellian way we can say that free will does not exist, but in order for society to run smoothly we must pretend that it does. Vacca discusses the ramifications from this doublethink and concludes that whether free will is an illusion or not depends on your point of view. Your free will is obvious, but that of others has to be taken on their say so.

It might be noted that free will, like religion, is adaptive in the Darwinian sense in that it has made the tribe more cohesive and effective.

Here's an example of Vacca's sometimes strikingly expressive prose: "As much as free will exposes humans to the threat of unlimited retaliation for wrong-doing, it nevertheless compensates them by making them the lords of their little domains, the micro-gods of their minds." (p. 394)

A very nice expression is Schopenhauer's: "Man is free to do what he wills, but he cannot will what he wills."

Near the end of his book *Life! Why We Exist...* Martin G. Walker acknowledges that free will may very well be an illusion. Nonetheless, he points out, it is an illusion that we cannot help but entertain. And then he makes a nice argument to see free will as "the ability to resist and turn away from the instinctive, natural but nonconscious striving...," adding, "Free will means simply a will freed of the constraints of the nonconscious..." (p. 119)

Quantum indeterminacy

Some people think that quantum indeterminacy allows free will. But it doesn't, mainly because quantum events in the brain (should there be any) are already resolved from indeterminacy before they can affect the neurological processes of the brain. Furthermore, if quantum indeterminacy did somehow affect the brain, we still wouldn't have free will, rather something more like random noise. What quantum indeterminacy does, however, is make it clear that a strict determinism regarding the universe is not tenable.

Christianity

In Christianity we have forgiveness. In a sense this can be seen as the subconscious knowledge (or symbolic expression) of the fact that we do not have free will. This is another example of religion as psychology. "Forgive them Father for they know not what they do." This is seldom interpreted as a statement supporting the idea that we do not have free will, but it could easily be, especially if you take it literally. The Son of God says we are not responsible. One way we are not responsible is that we do not have free will.

Again free will is an illusion we can't help but believe.

What causes a decision to be made?

To really get to the nitty-gritty of the conundrum it is perhaps better to say that for all the evidence we have it appears there is no reason to think that there is an "I" who is making independent decisions. And what would an independent decision be based on? How is a free will decision different from a random decision? If I say I have decided to take a nap, implied in this decision is the desire to take a nap or perhaps the need to take a nap. If it is desire, what causes that desire to arise? If it is need, what causes that need? If it is neither, then why did I decide to take a nap?

If I decide not to eat a second piece of chocolate fudge cake, this would appear to be a decision that goes against whatever is usually driving me. But why did I make this decision? Because I don't want to get fat? Because I want to show I have self-control? Because I want to eat some more cake later? Notice that again there is the necessity to ask, what is it that is driving me not to get fat? What is it that makes me want to demonstrate self-control?

It would appear that belief in free will requires a ghost in the machine or an endless regression into the past looking for causation.

So the first problem: who is this "I" who is said to be making these free-will decisions?

And the second problem is how can you tell that this "I" is making the decisions and not all the inputs to the I from sensory experience, from education and indoctrination, from the demands of the species mechanism?

Causation is also a mystery

I present this little digression about free will to make a point: we don't even know what free will is or if it could possibly exist. It's a human construction. In a mechanistic, even if organic, universe there is a rigid cause and effect relationship to events at the macro level. In such a universe free will is not possible. To make free will possible we have to allow that there are actions that are not caused by prior events—because if your behavior is the result of forces acting on you and your reaction to those forces, there is no free will involved.

How can we talk about free will when we don't even know what causation is?

Neuroscientist Rodolfo Llinas is talking about systems in the brain. He says:

There are two large systems: the more primitive one, the one of passions, pain, what a passion is, envy, sloth, lust, eating, and feeling. This is not negotiable. You like someone or not, something gives you pleasure or not, like a reptile. The possibility of negotiating with reality only occurs with the second system, the one of the neocortex, though it is completely dominated by the passions.
—in Margulis, Lynn and Eduardo Punset *Mind, Life, and Universe: Conversations with Great Scientists of Our Time* (2007)

Cognitive dissonance

Our minds don't work the way we think they do. Our limbic system compels us to do something. We imagine that we have made a decision to do whatever it is that our primitive brain has compelled us to do. We rationalize this compulsion and do it, or we do it and then rationalize it. We justify in rational terms why we are going to do something or why we have done something. This rationalization is essential for psychological homeostasis. If we can't rationalize the behavior in some way, then we can't do it, or if we have already done it, we are ill at ease in regret or guilt. We experience *cognitive dissonance*, which is intolerable. To return to a comfortable psychological homeostasis we can disremember what we did, we can deny that we did it, or we can pretend we didn't do it, etc. Sometimes we can simply say, it was a mistake, forget it, and move on. The important point is that our minds do not work toward an objective consideration of what we are going to do or have done, but work only toward a rationalization of what we are going to do or have done.

Society can help or hinder us in this. If society greatly condemns what we have done, then denial may be our only option. If society fosters the behavior we may be able to rationalize doing something that we would otherwise not do (such as kill a gook for God).

Superorganisms

We are superorganisms. Each one of the trillions of cells that make up our bodies is itself a living, metabolizing organism. Each cell is enormously complex, more complex than a Boeing 747 or a battleship. Each one of these cells communicates in some way with other cells so that the body has its community wisdom or swarm intelligence. The ego-I that thinks it is running the show really just expresses the combined expression of all those cells, which, by the way, are organized into organs, glands, muscles, neurons, etc. This is not to mention the trillions of microbes that live on or in our bodies which have their influence as well.

The statement "I have free will" falls apart first because of the "I." There is no independent "I" and there is no "I" that exists continuously over time. The illusion of free will is however all powerful, and the illusion is good enough. For life outside of philosophy it is as good as the real thing.

The ant colony decides to move. The workers pack up the eggs and the queen and they move. The ant colony has free will. It could decide to move or not. But no, ant colonies do not have free will. Who is it in the ant colony that makes the decision? Who exercises this free will? An ant colony is a superorganism. It operates through what is called swarm intelligence. What each member of the colony does is independent of hierarchal control. Each individual does its own thing. However each individual is influenced by what other individuals are doing. In a school of fish or a swarm of flying birds one often sees every single fish or bird turn in the same direction almost simultaneously. Each individual is reacting to what nearby individuals are doing. There is some trigger to turn left or right or up or down and zoom! they go almost as one.

In ant and bee colonies there is a division of labor. Members of the colony have different tasks based on their age or other factors. They do their tasks based on certain triggers such as pheromones, temperature, humidity, sunlight, darkness, etc. They operate automatically. They are also influenced by what the others are doing. If there is not enough activity going on in the midden pile, for example, some ants might start carrying out debris to the midden pile. If the temperature of the hive starts to rise some bees might start to flap their wings to generate air flow to cool off the hive.

In the human it is the same. We are superorganisms as well. There is no entity within us that makes a decision to do something or not to do it. There is the illusion of having made up our mind to do something or not to do it, but that always comes after the fact of the decision as Libet showed.

Chapter Eleven:

Infinities

Philosophy is the talk on a cereal box.

—Edie Brickell, "What I Am"

Beyond our ability to understand

Everything breaks down at the extremes including our logic and our science.

Like the reach of our eyes and our ears, our comprehension grows fuzzy at the extremes.

It is important to understand that this truth applies to everything: not only to very complex computer programs or to life forms doing extreme things, but to ideas as well. When the human mind uses words like "infinity," "determinism," "free will," "idealism," etc., the human mind is talking about things that it cannot fully understand. Our understanding of determinism for example works okay when what we are talking about is a closed system with a small number of variables. But when we apply determinism to our lives, we are applying it to the entire universe. We not only have no way of knowing all the events that led up to any given event, we have no way of knowing if there are not events involved that are beyond the reach of not only our ability to know but our ability to understand.

Consider that the universe may involve events at extremes so far away in time and space that we have never seen anything similar: particle physicists frankly tell us that before the Planck time they do not have a physical theory at all. And as far as infinities go, we have some understanding of what they are in mathematical terms; indeed we could say we understand infinities mathematically. But whether there are infinities in the universe aside from mathematical ideas is unknown and is in fact something physicists work hard to avoid. Finally, the universe itself after a very long—unimaginably long—time dissipates into the infamous heat death. Eventually every quark in the universe drifts so far apart from every other quark that they are invisible (if they could be seen in the first place!) to each other.

So does two plus two equal four?

Does two plus two equal four? Or better yet, is it possible that two plus two—somewhere, somehow, from some point of view—does not equal four?

This is a deep philosophical question. It is similar to the query about whether God can square the circle or do "impossible" things like move an immovable object. More generally speaking, is our logic sound and does its reach include all of the cosmos?

We like to think so, but in the world of quantum mechanics, which is a world more fundamental than the one in which we live, perhaps not. Two plus two equals four is a statement of logic or mathematics, which is pretty much the same thing. Our minds cannot conceive an answer to the question other than four. For us God cannot square the circle or be simultaneously the irresistible force and the immovable object. Nothing can go faster than the speed of light—well, according to inflation theory, the expansion of space apparently can. Who created God? Did God create God or has God always been?

Paradox

We have seen in various paradoxes, such as those of Zeno that expressing things verbally leads to contradictions that cannot be resolved. Expressing things mathematically is much more precise but as Gödel, Russell and other others have shown, even mathematics is not free of unavoidable contradictions. This all comes under the heading of everything breaks down at the extremes. Here's an exchange from John Horgan's book, *The End of Science: Facing the Limits of Knowledge in the Twilight of the Scientific Age* (1996):

"What's beyond the brick wall?"

"But that's Cartesian space, and even if space is curved you still can't help thinking about what's beyond the curve, even if that's not the right way of thinking about it." (p. 125)

Some ideas are not fathomable

This is the bugaboo of our minds, honed by the process of evolution: certain ideas are not fathomable no matter how hard we try (e.g., thinking of quantum mechanics).

It is impossible to think about the cosmos without having our notions tinged with the infinite. After all, it is hard to escape from the idea that the universe came from nothing or has always been. If it's always been, then that is infinity; and if there was once nothing, for how long was there nothing?

Infinity is not a number, but an idea.

There is a strange disconnect that exists between the idea of infinity in physics and in mathematics. In mathematics the idea of infinity is right there inescapably at the very beginning since there is no end to the integers. "One, two, three—infinity" so said George Gamow, and so it is unavoidably true. But in physics there still exists something like a horror of infinity so much so that should an infinity come up in the equations, it is considered a sure sign that something is wrong! Indeed, if I am reading the frustrating history of string theory correctly, it would appear that physicists are more comfortable with notions of upwards of 11 dimensions than they are with infinities.

The problem I think is that, although the mind of humanity cannot avoid the idea of infinity, in the physical world about us there is no proof of anything infinite. The grains of sand can be (in theory) counted. So too can the stars—well, maybe. Contrary to what is often thought, physicists insist that energy and matter, time and space do have a limit to their divisibility—the Planck limits. But I am guessing that even the carefully construed quanta of modern physics may prove to be divisible in ways at present incomprehensible to humankind. It wasn't so many years ago that it was thought that nothing existed beyond the Big Bang universe, or at least it was not considered "scientific" to speculate on such matters. Now we see eminent scientists speaking of a possible infinity of parallel universes, worlds forever beyond our ken. And it was only a little over a hundred years ago that the atom was thought to be indivisible.

The probability field

I think the problem that physicists are having in reconciling quantum mechanics and general relativity (string theory notwithstanding) is that the tool they are using to gauge the world of our senses, the world of "reality," the world of our instruments and even of imaginations, is infinite, while the "official" conception of that world is finite. The "tool" I am referring to is mathematics. The physicist's world in contrast is finite and discreet. There is a Planck limit on just how small that world can be subdivided, yet the tool of division is infinite. Quantum theory postulates that the world is not continuous, but composed of very small, discrete chunks, that is to say, quanta. One of the beautiful things about using quanta instead of a continuum is that the infinities are avoided. However, it has become increasingly obvious that quantum theory is not a complete, "final" theory mainly because nobody has been able to make gravity behave at the quantum level.

My "solution," which I hereby freely offer to the world, is to put the probabilistic uncertainty found in the behavior of quantum into a substratum that I call the "probability field." This is the ether returned with a vengeance. Instead of speaking of the wave properties of the photon, speak of the wave properties of the probability field. When the photon, for example, disturbs the underlying substratum so that a wave (defined probabilistically) goes out toward the slits, what is moving is not the photon, but the field itself. The probabilistic field is real. It is made up of some as yet undefined and undetected (and perhaps undetectable "substance"). Matter and energy disturb the probability field in characteristic ways. The disturbance in the field is what goes through the slits and it goes through in a way defined by the possibilities.

This field, unlike the current conception of space and time, does not have a quantum nature. One cannot say that there is a limit to its subdivision. Like the probability theory that describes it, it is infinitely divisible. Currently the fit between probability theory, which allows an infinite range of probabilities, from 0 to 1, and the field of space and time, which does not, is not good. We can always come up with a less and less likely event. If I describe an event that has a probability of happening of one over a googolplex, you can always describe an event even less likely as one half over a googolplex, and ad infinitum.

Infinitely divisible

So to correspond to our mathematics, space and time must also be infinitely divisible. The probability field must therefore be capable of being curved to a vanishingly fine degree. This "magic" world that our physicists have constructed where the division stops at the Planck limit is really just a convenience for their equations. Physicists understandably become frustrated and stymied when confronted with equations that involve infinities (that they cancel out). Sorry guys, but we can't limit the world of our senses and our imaginations by our inadequacies in math.

I came upon this conception because I have long been troubled by the way events are described in a probabilistic manner, for example Brownian motion. The motions of the molecules in the air are described in such a way that it is theoretically possible (although the probability is amazingly small) for all the molecules in this room to end up on one side. If I shoot a gun at the wall, the probability that I will hit that wall from a few feet away is very high, something very close to 1. Yet there exist just the very tiniest of tiny possibilities that the bullet will not hit the wall, but will describe a trajectory out of the barrel of the gun and back into my face! For the probability field to allow for these incredibly unlikely events, the field must be able to bend its shape to an infinite degree of fineness.

The probability field that the bullet travels through in the substratum must be shaped in such a way as to allow for the faintest of probabilities. A field described by discreet chunks would never be fine enough.

There would always be some aspect of the remotely possible that could not be accommodated. Ergo the field must be infinitely divisible and not composed of discreet quanta.

    Descends soapbox and exits stage

Chapter Twelve:

Doubt and the 10,000 Things

Doubt thou the stars are fire;
Doubt that the sun doth move;
Doubt truth to be a liar;
But never doubt I love.

> —Shakespeare, *Hamlet*

Everything breaks down at the extremes

It is important to understand (as any engineer does) that everything breaks down at the extremes. Just as the horizon endlessly retreats in front of the running man, so does the truth of our existence.

I saw a man pursuing the horizon;
Round and round they sped.
I was disturbed at this;
I accosted the man.
"It is futile," I said,
"You can never..."
"You lie," he cried.
And ran on.

> —Stephen Crane

"Ultimate reality" retreats from us as does the horizon.

Mathematics is a language

Mathematics may seem a bedrock, an eternal truth that cannot be denied. Two plus two equals four. How can that be denied? In any conceivable universe two plus two must equal four. Two things. Count them. Two more things. Count them. One, two, three, four. Yet mathematics breaks down at the extremes, or in fact before the extremes. Division by zero is not defined. Not defined! This is a cheesy way of saying we have no idea what it means to divide by zero. How nice it would be to have the inversion of multiplication by zero be consistent with the rest of the operations. Two times three equals six. Six divided by three equals two. Zero times three equals zero. (Multiplication by zero, note, however, *is* defined.) Three divided by zero equals...? We don't know. We can guess that it equals infinity. How many times will zero go into three? But "infinity" is not a number. It's an idea. By the way, zero divided by any number is still zero, unless of course it is divided by zero. Then it is undefined.

Mathematics in the final analysis is a language. Humankind's most precise language to be sure, but a language nonetheless.

Postmodern mathematics?

So, we *can* doubt the truth and/or the universality of mathematics. Although I find a lot of fault with the postmodern position on science and things that go bump in the night, I think the postmoderns have done us all a service by noticing that mathematics is a human construct and as such does not necessarily apply to the entire universe, and in fact its grand artifice may be defective in ways we do not and cannot know.

Shocking?

I think so.

Let me call up Tobias Dantzig who wrote *Number: The Language of Science* which first appeared in 1930. Here are a couple of quotes from that book to give you an idea of his position. By the way, Einstein called this "the most interesting book on the evolution of mathematics which has ever fallen into my hands." High praise indeed.

"[M]odern science differs from its classical predecessor: it has recognized the anthropomorphic origin and nature of human knowledge. Be it determinism or rationality, empiricism or the mathematical method, it has recognized that man is the measure of all things, and that there is no other measure." (p. 341)

Or more pointedly from a couple of pages earlier: "Man's confident belief in the absolute validity of the two methods [mathematics and experiment] has been found to be of an anthropomorphic origin; both have been found to rest on articles of faith."

These are inescapably the statements of a postmodernist. I was surprised to read them in a book on the theory of numbers, and even more surprised to realize that if mathematics is a distinctly human language, it is entirely possible that beings from distant worlds may speak an entirely different language; and therefore our attempts to use what many consider the "universal" language of mathematics to communicate with them may be in vain.

And this thought makes me wonder. Is the concept "two," for example, (as opposed to the number "2") really just a human construction? Would not intelligent

life anywhere be able to make a distinction, just as we have, between, say, two things and three things? And if so, would they not be able to count? And would not then the entire edifice of mathematics (or at least most of it) follow?

I wonder if Dantzig was not in contradiction with himself on this point because earlier he writes (p. 252) "...any measuring device, however simple and natural it may appear to us, implies the whole apparatus of the arithmetic of real numbers: behind any scientific instrument there is the master-instrument, arithmetic, without which the special device can neither be used nor even conceived."

Does this not imply that measurements (by any beings) and therefore numbers have an existence outside of the human mind and do not rest on "articles of faith"?

A yearning to divide by zero

Infinity, as we saw in the previous chapter, is an idea, the kind of idea from which there is no escape. What comes before the beginning? Nothing? What comes before nothing? Lots and lots of nothing. How far does this nothing stretch? For eternity. It has an endless expanse.

How many people in cyberspace have the screen name "dividesbyzero"? "Divides by Zero" appears on T-shirts. There is a vast yearning to divide by zero.

I think the problem is that zero like infinity is not a number. It is an idea, the absence of a number. It is a placeholder, and we have confused the placeholder with a number.

Write down the largest number. Sing the song the sirens sang. Get with child a mandrake root. Tell me where the past years are and who cleft the devil's foot. (Recalling John Donne.)

The substantive "nothing"

Read this twice: "Nothing ever remains the same." The first time read it with the understanding that everything is in flux, the second time read it realizing that if there is such a thing as "nothing" it is eternal and unchanging.

It is hard to talk rationally about something that is beyond rationality.

Cartesian doubt

Descartes proved to his own satisfaction that he exists. Actually he assumed it. As soon as he said "I think" he had already assumed his existence. The "think" is superfluous. One could say "I... therefore ...I" or simply "I" and achieve the same thing.

But Descartes did not prove to me that he exists. After all he could be just part of my construction of the world inside my mind. In fact, I cannot prove anything other than I exist. I cannot prove that I exist as a man or that I live on a planet called earth. All of the apparent facts of my existence may be just constructions, imaginings. I could be a great god who is having a dream. I am dreaming that I am a kind of creature that eats other creatures. Because I am a great god, my dream is amazingly vivid and amazingly detailed, right down to ideas about DNA and nuclear energy about which the character I have constructed (Dennis Littrell) has limited knowledge. This is called in philosophy "solipsism."

Solipsism could be true. It is also possible, according to the laws of thermodynamics that a tornado may appear and help to carry my house not to Oz but to Timbuktu. The odds against this happening are on the order of several googolplexes of googolplexes to one, I would guess; but it is not an impossibility in the same sense that squaring the circle is an impossibility.

A subjective sense of what is agreeable

Which brings me to my transition from Cartesian doubt to probabilistic doubt. Since nothing (other than I exist) can be established (and that is actually a given) how are we to say we know anything? The answer is we know things by their *perceived* likelihood of being true, by again perceived probability. Or more exactly by what *seems* more likely.

Understand this is not a necessary rule or a law or anything proven. It is like Occam's Razor: it is something that seems agreeable to my mentality.

Is it more likely that I am a great god dreaming I am a man, or is it more likely that I am actually a man? Occam's Razor would suggest the latter. My sense of what is likely would suggest the latter. My sense of what is agreeable to my mind suggests the latter. (Or maybe it doesn't.)

Consequently, instead of certain knowledge I am guided by "agreeableness," by what subjectively seems more likely.

This is of course entirely unsatisfactory for those who would like to have proof. Unfortunately for their desire, a subjective sense of what is probable is all we ever have. In fact, it is worse than that. It is almost better to say that a subjective sense of what is agreeable is all we ever have.

This may not seem to be getting us anywhere. As far as certain knowledge goes, as far as the ultimate nature of reality goes, we indeed are no closer to knowing than we were when we started. However, as far as how to live goes (which is what the Buddha decided was the real question, and one that could in fact be answered) we have made a definite start.

Ten thousand to one

We have decided to believe what is true in terms of how agreeable the alternatives are to our sense of what is likely. Will the car start when I turn the key? Probably. How probably? Well, I don't really have the ability to be exact, but based on personal experience, the experience of others, and to a kind of dim idea about how such things work, I would estimate the probability at, call it, ten thousand to one.

For most decisions in life, having odds of ten thousand to one is sufficient for us to take it as true. The proposition, will the car start is answered by a highly probable yes.

Notice that in the Tao Te Ching there is the concept of "the ten thousand things." It is a way of saying something indefinitely very large, but not infinite, but large enough for human purposes. Notice that John Donne's poem "Song: Go and Catch a Falling Star" alluded to above refers, you may recall, to "ten thousand days and nights" ('til age snow white hairs on thee"). Notice that ten thousand days and night is something in excess of approximately thirty years. This is the traditional age of manhood. You have a little more than thirty years to be what you are to be. Beyond that is uncertainty and doubt. You are either too young or too old. Bottom line: ten thousand is a big enough number for everyday purposes. And yet we have gone beyond that.

Deductive and inductive truths

Is the earth round (or nearly so) rather than flat? Again the odds can be roughly calculated. From all I know, having never heard anyone but a crackpot say otherwise, and having read a long history about how it was realized that earth was round, and from realizing that a myriad of things in this world depend on the earth being round, etc., etc., I can conclude with an extraordinary degree of probability that the earth is round rather than flat. (Well beyond ten thousand to one.)

Did humans actually land on the moon? Going through the same kind of calculation of what I know and what I have read and heard from others, the answer is almost certainly. In fact, it's easy to judge that it is much, much more likely that my car won't start than that the whole moon walk thing was a hoax or otherwise untrue.

After we do this for a while we begin to realize that all knowledge is probabilistic and relative. Consequently all opinions are probabilistic. There is no such thing (as far as humans go) as certain knowledge. There are no absolute truths outside of closed systems such as mathematics or logic. Two plus two equals four is an absolute truth but trivial since it can be derived from the definitions of "two," "plus" and "equals." This is an example of the difference between deduction and induction. Deductive truths really are true whereas inductive truths are always probabilistic, but unfortunately we don't know the universe of possibilities and therefore can never come to a true measure of probability.

But didn't I say that ALL truths are probabilistic? Yes. It is again possible—remotely—that some step in calculation inside a closed system is left out or added without our realizing it—or that we have a misunderstanding of the definitions (or axioms) or that somehow we have made a mistake. Consequently, even knowledge within closed systems is only probabilistic. The probability that two plus two is not four is on the order of the googleplex to the googleplex to the googleplex...to one, I would guess. At any rate, the probability is so low, we can treat the statement as though it were absolutely true.

The danger of absolute knowledge

Note here a guideline: when the odds are astronomical, it really doesn't make any difference whether the odds are two billion quadrillions to one or just one billion quadrillions to one. In both cases for most purposes the odds are identical.

We are limited creatures with a limited understanding of the world, and with a limited capacity for understanding the world. "Close" for us is the same as "exactly" in many cases.

All of this is not satisfactory. (Again the Buddha came to the conclusion that life is unsatisfactory.) We want certain knowledge. We yearn for the security of absolute truth. And therein is secreted a problem. Be sure that there are people who will attempt to meet our need for absolute truth. They can be very persuasive. They will invent gods and devils and great systems of religion and philosophy. They will invent infallible sources, usually sacred books or sacred men who got their knowledge from God. (They will even invent a God, of course.)

The problem with this is, once you know the "truth," once you have certain knowledge, there is no need to look any further. End of discussion. End of research. End of science.

Also some kinds of certain knowledge, such as how to behave, are in conflict with other kinds of certain knowledge. How can this be? It can't, so one side or the other (or both) must be wrong, or perhaps both right. This leads to conflicts, etc. Notice that uncertain knowledge, probabilistic knowledge, is less likely to lead to conflicts because no one is going to become violent because someone is saying that their very likely truth is in conflict with somebody else's very likely truth. It is likely that eating meat is immoral. It is likely that eating meat is moral. Since we don't know for sure, perhaps it is best not to kill one another over a difference of opinion.

A difference of opinion. Absolute knowledge does not allow a difference of opinion. Absolute knowledge is just that, absolute.

If that knowledge comes from God, then those who do not have that knowledge are at odds with God.

Morality is a human construct

Is abortion a bad thing? It depends on your point of view, on what you believe. It is a not a question of evidence per se because evidence (probabilistic knowledge) cannot answer such questions.

Science is just as good a basis for making moral judgments as is religion. Or just as bad.

What has followed in the past from taking science as the basis for moral authority is the idea that what is, is right. Nature is red in tooth and claw and therefore we should be also. Might makes right. Those who survive have the right morality, etc. This might be considered the purely "animal" view of morality. But this is a misunderstanding and misreading of nature, one that will be corrected in the years to come when the emphasis in evolutionary biology switches to a view based more on cooperation and working toward a symbiosis among living things as they create an ecology. Nonetheless, morality is a human construct and logically does not necessarily follow from any empirical observation.

Chapter Thirteen:

Nothing Is Real

Time

Time is an illusion. Neither time nor space exists independent of matter and energy.

Time only exists in terms of events. No events, no time.

When measuring time we always use some event as our source. Today we use events from cesium-based atomic clocks.

Here's Einstein on time from his famous paper "On the Electrodynamics of Moving Bodies" (1905) as presented in Stephen Hawking's book *A Stubbornly Persistent Illusion* (2007):

...[A]ll our judgments in which time plays a part are always judgments of simultaneous events. If, for instance, I say, "That train arrives here at 7 o'clock," I mean something like this: "The pointing of the small hand of my watch to 7 and the arrival of the train are simultaneous events." (p. 6)

From this it is apparent that Einstein did not believe that "time" has any existence outside of events, which necessarily take place using matter and/or energy. The fact that everybody including Einstein himself continued to talk as though time had some existence independent of matter and energy is just a convenience and a handy way of talking. In fact for Einstein time and space curiously are equivalent. They are spacetime.

Einstein does not say that time and space do not exist outside of matter and energy possibly because such a statement would be a metaphysical statement or something a philosopher might conjecture. It is not something that we would expect to be proved scientifically. However, physicist Carolo Rovelli (in *What We Believe but Cannot Prove* (2006), a collection of essays edited by John Brockman) is more explicit. He writes: "I am convinced, but cannot prove, that time does not exist..." (p. 229)

Time travel

The reason you can't go backward in time is that to do so everything that has happened since that point in time has to be undone, so to speak. The odds against that happening are...well, there are no words or even numbers that I can use to even hint at how unlikely that would be.

Traveling forward in time is, like the speed of light, a constant. But a machine taking us backwards in time is about as likely as...well, an impossibility. (But why should that stop us from dreaming? I like to imagine going back in time say 50,000 years to see America before there were any people here. How amazing the flora and fauna! Giant sloths and saber-toothed tigers, passenger pigeons flying overhead, obscuring the sun for hours!)

When physicists talk about the arrow of time going both ways it is a bit misleading since such possibilities are only available for particles in controlled, very small, and isolated environments. For the macro world time's arrow is as inexorable as the law of entropy.

Consider unscrambling an egg. How could that be done? Reversing time is reversing events. We cannot even begin to imagine how that might be done. And remember everything is connected to everything else, so to reverse "time" is to reverse all events in the universe.

Objective time (or mathematical time)

Surprisingly enough, philosophers are still not sure how to define objective time. (I'll just call it "time" for this section from here on out.) Time is like a river flowing. Time is like a snake with its tail in its mouth, cyclical. Time marches on; time has movement. Time is part of equations and is forever locked up with space as Einstein had it: spacetime. Time is a measurement relative to events. Or time measures the temporal order of events. Of course as Einstein showed, that order is a matter of where the observer is located relative to the events in question. Some events that we might like to compare in a "what came first" sort of way come down to a question of our position relative to the events (Einstein's relativity).

Time is a consequence of causality. The cause occurs before the event. The "before" seems to be a word that refers to something temporal, but actually it is a word that separates cause from effect. No passage of time should be implied. It is only the order of events we are talking about.

This brings me to a way of looking at objective time that I like very much: time as a mathematical point. Take away all the events that are ordered by cause and effect and what do you have? You have nothing. What is a mathematical point? It is an artificial construction that points to something that has no extension in any direction. It is a singularity. It doesn't exist in the real world. It exists only in the minds of people, mostly people who are physicists or mathematicians.

Time is a construct that we use as a tool to help us think about things, but has no existence outside of our constructions.

Psychological time

Psychological time is almost as illusive. Psychological time is subjective. It is something we experience as human beings. The days seem long when we are young, interminably so at times. But when we are old they fly by with increasing speed, until (some say, Jackson Browne for instance) at the very end, all of life is experienced as taking place in but the twinkling of an eye.

The main reason we experience time differently (and why psychological time exists) is that we experience life (events) differently at different ages, and at different moments in differing situations. For a child the day is very long because the child is doing so much during every second. For the child many events are entirely new; many things seen are seen for the first time. For those of us who are old we have had these experiences and have seen these things many times over. So we really don't experience them in the same way; we really don't see them. They pass us by almost imperceptibly. It is not only the child's mind and senses that are going full blast like the metabolism of a bird, but also the child's muscles and every cell in the child's body is doing so much more than they will some years later. Furthermore when the intensity of an experience is great so much more fully do we live it and that too stretches psychological time.

Birds live a year in a day. When I used to play basketball—full court strenuous basketball—ten minutes went by without the slightest sense of boredom, but the surprising thing was (and I experienced this most noticeably when I was in my middle years) after the game was over and I looked at a clock I was surprised at how little time had passed. While playing I was acutely aware of much of what was happening—so much happened in every second, players moving this way and that, the ball flying this way and that, my body responding and so on—so much happened in each second that each second seemed in retrospect that much longer.

Conversely when one is bored or has nothing to do, time drags. Is this a contradiction to what I just wrote? No, we are bored because our mind is focusing on all the things and feeling for all the things we are NOT doing. When we are doing something, paradoxically our mind slows down to concentrate on the task at hand. Notice that the young are the ones who are often bored. Older people—well, healthy older people—are seldom bored, mostly because we have learned to have something to do when time becomes available. The child only yearns for something he can't do at the moment and so the moment expands with his yearning.

Slowed-down time

When I first learned about Libet's half second delay in conscious awareness it seemed to explain the phenomenon we have of slowed-down time during some dramatic events. I recall returning home on the busy 605 Freeway in Los Angeles one day when a big white Cadillac about fifty feet or so in front of me spun out for some reason. I watched as the vehicle actually spun to straddle the entire lane, poking into the other lanes very busy with cars. Everything seemed to slow down as though I was watching in slow motion. Just as it appeared that the Cadillac would be hit, triggering a huge accident with me right in the middle of it, the Caddy spun back into the lane, and the car in the other lane and I just missed it. It seemed that I could see every detail. I was terrified of course and couldn't stop shaking afterwards for several minutes.

In Max Brockman's book *What's Next?: Dispatches on the Future of Science* (2009) there is an essay by neuroscientist David M. Eagleman entitled "Brain Time" in which Eagleman addresses this familiar phenomenon that "time 'slows down' during brief, dangerous events such as car accidents and robberies." (p. 159) What Eagleman confirmed is that because of the emergency situation we take in much more information about what is happening than we usually do and this "higher density of data" makes the event appear to last longer." (p. 161)

Space

Space also appears to depend on matter/energy to have any meaning.

What is the distance from nowhere to nowhere? What is the distance from nothing to nothing? The arguments against time's independent existence apply in similar form to space.

However, I think it's fairly clear that space does exist much like the ether of old. I believe this because there has to be a medium out of which the virtual particles of the uncertainty principle appear, and because space is apparently expanding.

Nothing

One of the curious consequences of the uncertainty principle from quantum mechanics is that "nothing" is not nothing anymore. The vacuum of space ("nothing") is not entirely empty, and in fact cannot in principle ever be empty. As physicist John D. Barrow explains in *The Book of Nothing: Vacuums, Voids, and the Latest Ideas about the Origins of the Universe* (2000) it would be a violation of the uncertainty principle for space to be entirely empty. This is because "If we could say that there were no particles in a box, that it was completely empty of all mass and energy," we would have "perfect information about motion at every point and about the energy of the system at a given instant of time." (from Chapter 7, "The Box that Can Never Be Empty," p. 204).

This rather simple, but shocking revelation, has consequences that are shaking the very foundation of our understanding of the cosmos. Quite simply it appears that there is no such thing as nothing.

A kind of Zen enlightenment

This leads us to my favorite philosophic question, "Why is there something rather than nothing?"

When I first asked myself this question many years ago I experienced a kind of Zen enlightenment. It was Wow! The whole universe seemed to expand, open up and zoom out to infinity as my mind raced toward the answer. But there was no answer.

Since then I have learned that this question has been asked many times by people such as Stephen Hawking who phrased it this way: "Why does the universe go to all the bother of existing?" He believes that if we do discover a complete Theory of Everything, a TOE—the holy grail of modern physics—we will then be able to answer this question, and then we will "know the mind of God." (*See The Theory of Everything: The Origin and Fate of the Universe* (2002))

Physicist Richard Morris asks the question in his book, *The Big Questions: Probing the Promise and Limits of Science* (2002). He gives credit to Gottfried von Leibniz for first posing the question three hundred years ago (p. 9); but trust me, it was asked long before Leibniz ever existed.

It is to me the most fundamental of all questions and the most mystifying. Just asking the question is an enlightenment—at least it was for me when I was a young man. I asked the question and immediately was struck with how incredible any answer might be. The very fact that there is something rather than nothing seemed amazingly miraculous; and in fact the real lesson of asking the question is that it provides a hint, just a hint, of how stupefying to our feeble minds everything is, and how far we are from understanding more than the tiniest bit of what there is to know.

The question worked for me as a Zen koan. It seemed that by being able to pose such a question I had proven the existence of God. (Which might suggest how easy it is for our minds to posit a God from no evidence at all.) Not the sort of God most people talk about. No this God was more like the God of the Vedas about which nothing can be said.

I don't mean "proven" in the scientific sense or even in a sense that would be meaningful for anyone else. I suspect my experience was similar to that of Descartes when he thought he had proven that he existed when he said, *ergo cognito sum*. Of course, as pointed out in the previous chapter, he had proven nothing since to say "I think" is to assume a thinker, linguistically speaking, at any rate.

By the way, here are some other important books I've run across in which this question is asked:

Susskind, Leonard *The Cosmic Landscape: String Theory and the Illusion of Intelligent Design* (2005)
Taylor, John. *When the Clock Struck Zero: Science's Ultimate Limits* (1992)
Trefil, James. *101 Things You Don't Know about Science and No One Else Does Either* (1996)
Walker, Martin G. *Life! Why We Exist... And What We Must Do to Survive* (2006)
Wilson, Edward O. *On Human Nature* (1978)

Some possible answers:

1. Nothing is impossible (from QM).
2. Something is more "natural" than nothing (from Victor Stenger in his book *Quantum Gods*).
3. The concept of nothing is meaningless without the concept of something (my "verbal" argument).
4. There is something rather than nothing because there is no such thing as nothing (again from QM).

This makes me think that the old bugaboo about the universe having no beginning or being created from nothing is no longer such a quandary because (1) nothing is something; and (2) nothing has always been here. In other words, the question is answered: the universe (or mega-universe or super-universe, or whatever) had no beginning and is eternal.

And so, here are two quotations proving once again that the deepest truths known to humankind can be found in popular song lyrics:

"Nothing is Real." —The Beatles, "Strawberry Fields Forever" (It really is real!)

"Nothing really matters." —Freddy Mercury (of Queen), "Bohemian Rhapsody" (It does indeed!)

Chapter Fourteen:

Religion

Religion is the smile on a dog.

—Edie Brickell, "What I Am"

A God beyond logic

A God about whom nothing can be said was the choice of the Vedic ancients. They wanted a God beyond logic, a God that had this attribute: whatever you said about God would not apply in any way. *Neti, neti, neti*: not this, not this, not this.

There are no guarantees that such a God exists, but then again it could be said that such a God is beyond the duality of existence and non-existence.

A supernova to a candle flame

The first mistake is to say anything at all about God.

God is ineffable. Anything we can say about God is bound to be wrong. Not this, not this, not this. God is so beyond any human comprehension as to be like a supernova to a candle flame. And that is an understatement, and indeed I've already violated the rule. The only thing to say about God is nothing. Like the Buddha, keep a strict silence about God.

The second mistake is to presume to speak for God.

This is a most grievous error. There can be no excuse for something like this. A good rule is, if you ever hear anyone presuming to speak for God, run the other way, and fast.

The third mistake is to imagine that God has chosen your ear in which to whisper.

God is the ocean of information that comprises all that is or ever will be or ever could be, and beyond that because to limit God to our ideas of what could be is silly. God is both the potential and the actual and even the impossible. God is everything I can say about God and more and less and not even that. Our words fail, our logic is too limited. We cannot measure the ocean of Brahman with the teacup of our mind.

This the Buddha saw in his meditations and finally said Stop!

We are like the ant

The ant does not know, although it may walk upon the pages of the *Wall Street Journal*, the price of a share of General Electric. It may have a crude sense of price, feeling within its system the cost of carrying a grain of rice for a hundred meters. So we too sense space and time, but it is a sense conditioned and shaped by our evolutionary past and our evolutionary needs and the limits of our senses and instruments and imagination. A greater realization of space and time is as obtuse to us as are the black markings on the pages of the *Wall Street Journal* to the ant that so energetically scurries over them.

Science is a tool that can very often give us the answer, the highly probable answer, and lead to a plan.

But this is not necessarily good enough for many humans, psychologically speaking. They want absolute truth, which science can never provide. Only an all-powerful God can provide absolute certainty, and so humans often choose the absolute certainty of a putative God to the highly probable truth of science. As usual, habits of mind and the limbic system trump rationality.

By the way, technically speaking scientific truth is not "probable"; it is just the best choice that we have. Philosopher David N. Stamos (*Evolution and the Big Questions* 2008) called science "the inference to the best explanation." Probability as a mathematic concept, and in information theory, can be defined precisely, but in the real world it remains a mystery. We don't really understand probability because we don't have the universal set from which to derive the likelihood of events; furthermore, we are not sure what "random" means. Again "random" can be defined in information theory, but what is a random event in the cosmos? We don't know.

Superstition

People will believe in things not in evidence, such as God, because the brain needs to create a sense of control in the face of uncertainty and lack of control. When we are ignorant about what is going on, such as was primitive man in the eye of the storm, or in the throes of a disease, if we believe, however erroneously that we have some control, that we understand that God is working in his wondrous ways, etc., this is better than pure despair. It is like the placebo effect. If we believe we have some control, this is better than non-belief even if our belief is entirely specious. This phenomenon leads to not just our belief in a God, and in particular a personal God who is looking out for us, but to belief in *sympathetic magic*. Belief in bogus things has survival value in some situations and is therefore an adaptive trait of humans. In other words, in some situations self-deception is will help us survive.

The most superstitious people are those in circumstances in which they feel they have limited control. In baseball, where even the good hitters are successful only about 30% of the time and the ball can take funny bounces, players follow all sorts of superstitious acts such as not stepping on the foul lines, eating only chicken the day of a game (Wade Boggs), touching themselves in various ways before batting, perhaps going through certain pre-batting rituals. When I young and played poker in the California card rooms, as I was driving into the Los Angeles basin on the freeway, I would look at the license plates of other cars for signs of good hands. A license plate such as 556 ACA would be two pair, aces and fives. If I found a plate with four of a kind, I would consider it a good omen. I would do this even though I knew it had absolutely no effect on what cards I would be dealt.

Sympathetic magic

Farmers and agrarian people in general, hunters and gathers, and others close to the earth and sky follow a myriad of rituals and practices that they feel will help with the harvest, the weather, the abundance of game, etc., rituals and practices that as a scientific matter have nothing to do with increasing rainfall or attracting game or scaring away locusts. Such practices fall under the general umbrella of sympathetic magic which ironically is the precursor of science.

When things are out of control, when there are many factors that affect our wellbeing about which we know little or nothing and over which we have little or no control—when the wind rages and the earth shakes, when the parched land cries out for rain, what can be done? To do nothing is to feel helpless. But to perform a rain dance or to sacrifice a goat, or to chant sacred words is to do something rather than nothing, and in doing this (especially if we believe it may be effectual), we gain some control over our lives; and instead of just giving up, we have the strength to continue for another day or so. And in doing so, we may very well survive while those who give up all hope are more likely to die.

Four reasons people believe in a personal God

Consequently people who believe in a personal God who is looking out for them gain what might be called the placebo effect advantage over those who do not. I don't recall what the percentage of cases in which a placebo has proven effective, but I know that it is a non-trivial percentage.

Another reason that belief in a personal God is adaptive is that having a God that is powerful and looks out for us increases our sense of self-worth. If the All Mighty cares about us, we must be of some real value.

A third reason is that belief in a personal God serves to give purpose and direction to our lives. Our purpose is to serve God or at least do what God wants us to do. Psychologically speaking, people have greater strength when they believe they are working together with others for a common purpose, and working with God toward doing his will is easily seen as a very fine purpose indeed.

A fourth reason that belief in a personal God is adaptive is that when everybody in the tribe believes in a great leader like God (and/or his ministers) this brings cohesion to the tribe and allows the tribe to act more effectively. All the tribes that did not have a personal God or some sort of supernatural organizing and motivational being to follow, died out. Today all the people in the world are descended from people who believed in some kind of supernatural power that rallied the tribe's strength and got its young men to give their lives in warfare for the good of the tribe.

That takes religion!

The idea that somebody is in charge, that somebody is behind whatever happens, that there is purpose and maybe even a plan, that there is meaning, etc., is built into our psyches. It is part of our having a "theory of minds" about others. Somebody is responsible. Therefore we have invented God, a kind of super human who is in charge, who is behind whatever happens, who has a purpose and a plan, and we are part of it!

However, physicist Steven Weinberg in his book, *Facing Up: Science and Its Cultural Adversaries* (2001) writes: "...on balance the moral influence of religion has been awful." He adds, "With or without religion, good people can behave well and bad people can do evil; but for good people to do evil—that takes religion." (pp. 241-242)

What is the purpose of life?

You know the quick answer: there is no purpose to life. Life is "a tale told by an idiot, full of sound and fury, signifying nothing." Those are Shakespeare's words and that is also the opinion of modern science. One can say with the existentialists that life has no purpose other than that which one superimposes on it.

But let's look at some other possible answers to the question. One could be to serve God. Well, any God worthy of the name would hardly need our service. Another might be to help our fellow person. This is better but it begs the question of why there might be a fellow person around that needs help in the first place. And what *is* the purpose of humans?

To the ordinary mind there is always a purpose, a plan, a goal. This is built into our nature as surely as sex and metabolism. When there is no goal, no purpose, no plan, our behavior becomes meaningless, random, senseless. So we superimpose meaning and purpose onto our lives, and there is nothing quite so efficacious as God for doing this. God is our purpose. God is the answer to what we do not know or understand. If God did not exist we would have to invent him (Voltaire), and so on.

Religion is also about paternity and psychology and war, and it's adaptive in the Darwinian sense (which is why we have it).

In religion is found the true psychology of humankind—or at least it was until the advent of cognitive psychology, evolutionary psychology, and modern neuroscience. Academic psychology prior to these three great advances was primitive compared to the wisdom found in the great religious traditions.

Why we need religion

We need religion because otherwise we would be completely beholden to the tribe and our biological nature. It doesn't matter whether religion is true or not. We need a higher authority than the church, the state or our biological nature.

At some point the individual must say no to society and to the dictates of the evolutionary mechanism. To do this comfortably, the individual, who is after all indoctrinated, socialized and at the mercy of his emotions, must have recourse to a higher power. If there isn't one, the individual must invent one. And *that* takes religion.

Chapter Fifteen:

Life and Death

We're in the universe and the universe is in us.

—Neil deGrasse Tyson

Vitalism

It is fashionable and psychologically compelling to believe that life is something miraculous, something deeply mysterious and strikingly different than anything else in the universe. The truth is that life is a natural and probably inevitable consequence of matter and energy. Given the right circumstances life will begin. We don't yet know how that happens, and it may be a long time before we get it figured out, but there can be no escape from the conclusion that life comes naturally from matter and energy and is not in essence different from matter and energy. To think otherwise is to conjure up the ghost in the machine, or more properly, a kind of dualism, invoking the vitalism of the 19th Century.

Vitalism is the idea that there is something vital within a life form that accounts for its being alive. You look into someone's eyes and you can't help but see that the person is alive! The intelligence and selfness sparkles out to you. But this is an illusion caused by the evolutionary mechanism which is full of illusions that serve us well in our struggle to survive and reproduce.

You will die

Life is a candle between two eternities of darkness.

You will die, but it won't matter because as far as you will ever know, you're always alive.

Besides, you weren't alive in the way you thought you were in the first place.

They say that life is but a candle in the wind between two vast eternities. But psychologically even a moment of this life is greater than all the eternity that came before. And you will never experience the eternity to come. You can only contemplate it—and to what advantage and to what end? Furthermore, you were not worried about nor in fear about anything in that vast eternity before you were born, and in this life you are not troubled by not existing during that unimaginably long period of time so long ago. So why should you stress about the eternity to come? And if indeed the universe is infinite in time and extent, eventually you will be born again in identical circumstances, but that (if true) may provide no comfort since you will not recall the present you and that very distant you will be in the same state of mind as the present you.

The "red slayer"

I was thinking about the vastness of the universe and the possible vastness beyond that and forward and backward in time, and realized that in a clockwork-like universe in which there is causality from one state of the universe to another, the present would imply the future in an entirely rigorous way, and so the future would be contained in the present just as the number four is contained in "two plus two."

(For the sake of this observation I am ignoring the uncertainty principle from quantum mechanics in which we learn that the universe *cannot* be seen in a strictly determinist way.)

A demigod, who could have complete knowledge of the state of the universe at a particular time, could theoretically foresee all that is to come. Therefore what is to come is eternal, just as what has come to past is eternal. I existed at the beginning of the universe, as did you. This is what Krishna means when he says, in the *Bhagavad Gita*: "Never was there a time when I did not exist, nor you, nor these lords of men, and never shall any of us cease to exist hereafter."

Ralph Waldo Emerson rendered this idea in his poem "Brahma," thus:

If the red slayer thinks he slays,
 Or if the slain think he is slain,
They know not well the subtle ways
 I keep, and pass, and turn again.

Beyond the ether

Furthermore, the "idea" that is me, the particular ensemble of elemental atoms made into molecules made into cells made into organs, was there in the beginning without manifestation, yet clearly both a possibility and a reality to come. Consequently all my ideas and all the things I have said and done were there too in the beginning. And all the potential I could have been. And they will be there after I "die." The atoms of my body will disperse, but the form and the interactions that have been my life will exist forever, somewhere beyond the ether, somewhere beyond time and space, and yet everywhere all at once.

Time is an illusion and space a mystery. Ultimate Reality is beyond our ken. It is remarkable that we can know this. And yet so little do we know relative to what there is to know.

A student said: "In the end we are all dead. There is no memory, no perception, no awareness of anything we ever did. So do any of our choices matter? Does morality matter?"

Morality may or may not matter at the level of philosophy, that is, as regards our understanding of ultimate truths or at the end of the imagined universe. But it sure does matter on the various levels of society, personal relationships, etc.

Implicit in the question is the notion that there is an end. I don't get depressed or feel that life is meaningless (as some people understandably do) when I think of the heat death of the universe because I can't imagine a time when there is nothing any more than I can imagine a time before today when there was nothing. The end of the universe as imagined by physicists is merely the end of a universe that physicists can be aware of.

Finally while there may be no memory in the atoms of my body which have scattered to become dust in the wind, there is always the possibility of something greater than humans, which I find comforting.

You should not fear death

It is natural to be afraid of death. I can recall just how scary death was when I was young. I can also recall how scary it was to imagine the world without me. How desolate it seemed! How lonely I felt. The world here and me nowhere. Emptiness. The void.

I am no longer afraid of death, and I will explain why. The explanation is subtle and difficult to appreciate at first hearing. It is like "an enlightenment" from an Eastern religion. When I gave this explanation to a friend, a very intelligent and learned man, he found no satisfaction in it and I said I understood. Most people who hear this find no satisfaction in it. But I am going to go ahead anyway.

Here is why you should not fear death. (I know I am repeating myself, but this bears repeating.)

You are always alive. You never die. Other people die. You experience other people's deaths, but you never experience your own. You can anticipate your death of course, and that is unpleasant, so don't do it.

You were "dead" for an eternity of darkness before you were born. Did that bother you? Does it bother you now?

Furthermore, we are not "alive" in the sense that we think we are. Fear of death is a trick of the evolutionary mechanism to make us more careful about protecting our reproductive opportunities. What we fear is the loss of identification, an identification with this mind and body.

Happy is the man who dies in his sleep. He does not anticipate his death. He is asleep. He dies. Before going to sleep he was awake and alive. Before the hearse comes and he is buried or cremated, the last thing he experienced was being alive. He never experienced his death. He was, to himself, never dead. So die as though in a deep sleep. As the tiger sinks its canines into your throat, smell the fur of the tiger, see the blue of the sky and the green of the trees.

Fear of pain

There is of course the fear of painful, violent death. But the fear is in the pain and the horror of violence. It is not in the death itself. It is what causes the death that you experience before dying.

"We hold that the individual dies with the death of the visible body; Indian religious systems hold as a core belief that the individual is not that which dies but is instead the forces which brought the body and personality into existence..." from the essay by Michael N. Naglar in *The Upanishads* edited by Eknath Easwaran, p. 287.

Death is nothing to us. For all good and evil consists in sensation, but death is deprivation of sensation. And therefore a right understanding that death is nothing to us makes the mortality of life enjoyable, not because it adds to it an infinite span of time, but because it takes away the craving for immortality. For there is nothing terrible in life for the man who has truly comprehended that there is nothing terrible in not living. —Epicurus

If young people knew how great it is to be old they would be jealous. But they are protected from that knowledge since to the young the old look wrinkled and spent and not attractive. And for the young those are important things.

Chapter Sixteen:

God and Unintelligent Design

The "argument" from a perceived probability

While there's no logical argument that proves the existence of God, there are some "interesting" ones, at least from a psychological perspective. Evolution has put a damper on the old argument from design, but the incredible, mind-boggling vastness of the universe as discovered in the twentieth century suggests what I might call "the argument from a perceived probability."

Three kinds of God

But first let's be clear about what we mean by "God." For the sake of convenience I'll give three different sorts of god that people talk about. There are others, of course.

First there's a being superior to us that may or may not have created the universe. It comes in two varieties. If it created the universe, it's the Creator God. If it is just a very superior creature with vast powers like Superman then we have the Superman God.

Another sort of God is the Personal God like the God of Christianity or Islam who intervenes in the world in wondrous and scary ways and has a lot of human characteristics like a bad temper and a need to be worshiped and obeyed.

A third God is a God beyond our understanding such as Brahman of the Vedas, a God about which nothing can be said or known.

The argument from (an unknown) probability would suggest that the Superman God certainly exists. Indeed there could be a lot of them. The universe is so grand that there must be creatures greater than us. It is also possible there is a God that created the universe in which we exist (a subset of a larger universe), perhaps for amusement or as an experiment or for reasons beyond our ken.

Unfortunately the argument from probability does nothing for a possible Personal God. More than anything a Personal God resembles an anthropomorphic projection of the human psychic, truly an all-powerful father figure.

And of course a God about which nothing can be said clearly seems not impossible.

The "argument" from faith

I also like an argument that I call the argument from faith. The argument from faith takes as a given that there is a limit to what we can know. At some point we all realize that there are things about life and death and the universe that we just don't and can't know. What to do? Cringe in doubt and insecurity? I think not. Have faith that there is something beyond us.

Obviously this is not a logical argument.

Purpose

When we talk about intelligence—human intelligence, animal intelligence—we are implying a purpose, a goal. We must always bear in mind the unstated question haunting the lofty idea of intelligence is "Intelligence for what?" The bird that flies on the wing has a great intelligence, the intelligence of flight.

"Purpose" is a human concept that we apply to our experience. The idea of "intelligence" has no meaning without the idea of purpose. Consequently when people speak of "intelligent design" they are in the very expression itself implying purpose. So in a sense what they are doing is assuming that which they would like to demonstrate, namely that the universe has a designer who had a purpose.

Purpose is purely anthropomorphic thinking and may or may not have the slightest application to the universe at large.

That is problem number one with the idea of intelligent design. Note that evolution—which the intelligent designers are trying to discredit and supplant—implies no such thing as purpose. This really is the crux of the debate. Intelligent designers cannot get beyond their unstated assumption of purpose. They have seen purpose in their lives; indeed all animals are involved in goal-oriented behavior. The purpose of behavior is to fulfill some goal. So their minds are uncomfortable with the idea of a purposeless universe. The idea that the universe is just here without rhyme or reason does not appeal to them. In fact they find such an idea intolerable, and so they look to discredit it.

Unfortunately there is no way purpose on a cosmic scale can be demonstrated scientifically. So what intelligent designers end up doing is nitpicking at biological evolution, trying to find holes and mistakes in the edifice while asserting that the universe is designed, implying a Designer. In no way does this approach allow for any sort of scientific testing or the possibility of being refuted. There will always be ways in which a scientific theory like biological evolution is incomplete or mistaken in some way, so errors will be found and misconceptions and the like. Regardless the edifice stands.

The main argument advanced to support creationism or Intelligent Design (better understood as UnIntelligent Design) is the venerable argument from design as mentioned above. A watch implies a watchmaker, etc. That argument has been refuted again and again, but like kudzu it pops up again and again. Intelligent designers look at an organism and say this is so beautifully and intricately designed that it must have a designer. It could never happen by chance. But of course an organism is not a watch and was not designed and constructed, but evolved. To assert that something is too complex for the evolutionary process to evolve is to assert human ignorance. Just because some humans can't imagine how something complex could have arisen through the process of evolution isn't much of an argument.

Chance

An organism implies no designer; indeed an organism can be understood as the product of the intrinsic nature of matter and energy, time and space. Chance is not involved at all. Indeed "chance" is another anthropomorphic notion that may or may not have any application in a cosmic sense. All of this is more or less understood in scientific circles. Unfortunately it is not understood by the populace at large.

Some intelligent designers are not capable of understanding anything beyond purpose. Other intelligent designers don't care in the slightest about the science one way or the other. They are only interested in overthrowing what they see as a noxious world view implied by biological evolution. They are interested in power. They want to stop any sort of science that goes against their world view. They want to replace the scientific method of evaluating truth with authoritarian truth. "The Bible said it, I believe it, and that settles it," sums up their world view. In Islam of course we see something similar: God, through his Prophet, set down the ways to live and that settles it.

Faith

A student wrote: The very concept of faith is believing in the unbelievable.

True. Additionally faith is believing even though you don't know or have no way of knowing, or believing even though the evidence is to the contrary.

I had to point out to another student that regardless of what your Muslim friends say and how nicely they behave toward you, remember they are practicing a religion that has as one of its basic tenets that death shall be given to anyone who leaves the faith. And other barbarisms of Sharia law are well known. Not to mention how few are the rights of women in Islam compared to the rights of men.

Of course a distinction between Islam as practiced in Saudi Arabia and say Malaysia should be noted.

Christianity would be just as bad except for the fact that predominately Christian nations have separation between church and state and so the power of the church is limited. Not so in Islam/Arabic lands, which are virtually all non-democratic. In Islam only God can rule; certainly not the people themselves.

Finally, the most valuable and meaningful distinction to make is not between the Abrahamic religions themselves, but between the fundamentalist and more progression expressions of those religions.

Faith begins where reason ends. And as Emily Dickinson sarcastically wrote many years ago:

"Faith" is a fine invention
When Gentlemen can see—
But Microscopes are prudent
In an Emergency.

In the Bush administration we had a faith-based foreign policy and a faith-based science policy, but the problem with that is "faith-based" is "ignorance-based."

Faith is fine in matters about which we can have no information. But when we have it, it is better to use that information rationally rather than to resort to a blind reliance on faith.

Religions as psychologies

I like to define religions as psychologies, that is, as guides on how to live and how to understand yourself and your place in the world, and especially how deal with the uncertainties of life, most especially the fact of death. The Buddha saw this very early on and devoted his life to teaching people how to live and so he put aside questions about God and the hereafter.

With the explosion of insights from neuroscience, cognitive psychology, and evolutionary psychology, this aspect of religion is becoming less significant.

Chapter Seventeen:

More on Religion

I got a friend in Jesus
So you know that when I die
He's gonna set me up with
The spirit in the sky.

— Norman Greenbaum, "Spirit in the Sky"

Does God exist? And if so, what is God's nature? Usually when you read questions like this in the United States you can prepare yourself for a "yes" and some glorious rendering of God as a kind of divine father in the sky who is watching over humans, a God who has a place for us in heaven, if only we will do the right thing.

All this is just pure poppycock. Whether God exists or not depends on how you define God. If you define God as the God of the Old Testament, then obviously God does not exist. Such a depraved, vengeful psychopath could only be a bogeyman from the dark depths of the human mind. If you define God as the creator of the universe, who did his thing and then went south (the deist position), then God may exist, but what good is He? We could just as well have the universe invent itself or be eternal in time with no beginning and, perhaps, no end.

If you define God as an entity beyond human comprehension about which nothing can be said, an entity that exists as the answer to all that we do not know, then such a God may indeed exist, and if he didn't exist we might want to invent him.

The idea of God, then is true, and does exist. God stands for all that we don't understand, all that we can't understand, all that is beyond our reach. Personally I believe in God, but not in God as God is usually imagined. The God that I believe in is a God about which nothing can be said. Anything you say about God gets an immediate nay. God is so beyond our comprehension, so beyond anything we can imagine that anything we can say about God is not even wrong. This God is the real thing. This is the God that really works in mysterious ways, ways so mysterious that we could never understand them even if there were some attempt to explain them to us. Can the ants that move along the pheromone trails understand algebra or human languages? We are like those ants in relationship to God, only more so.

Religion is about certainty

(Yes, I know I am repeating myself, but this bears repeating.)

People yearn for certainty. They want absolutes. They cannot abide swimming in the sea of uncertainty. That is why we invented God. The nice thing about God is that to true believers nobody is ever going to be able to prove that God does not exist. Even such a formulation of God as the Flying Spaghetti Monster is impossible to disprove simply because whatever scientific evidence is presented, believers can always say God makes it seem that way to fool unbelievers. (Logically this is similar to solipsism.)

156

Realizing this we can see that the purpose of God is to give believers certain knowledge that cannot be dispelled. That's why they call it faith.

Why should humans require this "certain knowledge"? Wouldn't it be better to go with what seems right from all that we can know empirically, in a scientific way, in a common sense way, by the report of our senses?

The trouble with this is that sometimes (and inevitably) there will come into the life of people unacceptable negativity such as the death of a loved one, such as a terrible debilitating disease or accident, such as defeat in war or economic failure, unlucky in love and cards, the rains don't come, the American electorate makes an idiot president, etc., etc. These calamities can be so depressing psychologically that the human may give into despair and just give up.

That would not be adaptive. But if one can believe in a heaven after this brief purgatory on earth, then maybe one doesn't give into despair. Or if one can believe that the evil doers—and there are always evil doers who play the role of scapegoats for our ills—if one can believe that these bad people will get their just deserts in the afterlife, then again one may not give in to despair. Or if one can believe that the bad people will come back as donkeys and we good people will be rewarded with a higher status in the next incarnation, then once again one need not give into despair.

God is the answer to all unanswered questions

So a belief in things not in evidence can be adaptive in an evolutionary sense. This is not the only way that religion is adaptive however. In the tribal society, in the long ago world of the warlords (still with us actually), getting young men to die for the good of the tribe was adaptive. The tribe that had a shaman who promised the young men heaven as their reward for killing members of the other tribe had an advantage over those tribes that failed to get their young men into the proper mood. Furthermore, religion and the shared belief in something greater than ourselves and in life after death and all the accouterments of religion made the tribe more cohesive.

So God is an adaptation to the war system environment that allowed its practitioners to outcompete the competition for resources, and that is why every society on earth has some sort of religion. Those tribes that did not, died out. God is therefore in our genes in the same way that lust and love are.

Well, some people don't seem to believe in God or an afterlife. Some people would not be willing to blow themselves up in order to frolic in heaven with virgins.

Yes, it is true that the genetic endowment of belief is not complete or uniform. But so it is with many other human traits. When and if the war system ends, after a long period of time in which belief in the supernatural is not rewarded in a Darwinian sense, the innate belief in gods and heaven and such will wane, and eventually there will be only a random scattering of such genes, or more properly, such combinations of genes.

Evolution and atheism

Evolution doesn't disprove God, but what it does disprove is the literal word of the Bible, as does physics.

I want to add that it is useful to make a distinction between atheism and agnosticism.

But first it is essential (as above) to define the God we are talking about. Richard Dawkins in *The God Delusion* admitted he really was an agnostic when it came to the deist sort of God. On page 51 he wrote that he identifies himself as among those who say, "I cannot know for certain but I think God is very improbable, and I live my life on the assumption that he is not here."

This may surprise some people, and perhaps even Dawkins himself who likes to profess his atheism. However that atheism only applies to certain kinds of God, for example, those that answer prayers.

What such a personal God is doing is allowing us finite creatures to share in His Glory by being the instruments of His infinite mercy. The fact that this may seem to amount to divine masturbation when you really think about it, should not deter us. One could just as easily think that the whole idea of creating beings like us to play with is divine masturbation, and we will have none of that!

Religion and language

I would also argue against Dawkins' meme theory in which he sees the delusive ideas of religion being replicated as by-products of our cultures. Many religious ideas do have a cultural basis, but the core ideas of religion such as gods, an afterlife, and a spiritual realm can be found almost universally and, even after lying dormant, these core ideas pop up again and again in different guises.

This suggests to me that religious ideas are innate in the same sense that our propensity for language is innate. Indeed, there are striking similarities between the propagation and the phenomenon of religion and that of language. Both are ubiquitous across cultures. And they are at their core similar in all cultures, but superficially different in specifics. Furthermore, there is plenty of evidence that people would as children invent a language if they had none; and we know that people invent religions all the time. Dawkins mentions Scientology and Mormonism as well as the cargo cult of the South Pacific as fairly recent examples.

One other point: Dawkins argues against using God as a creator because then we have to account for the creation of God. He says this results in an infinite regress unless we "make the entirely unwarranted assumption that God himself is immune to the regress." (p. 77) Putting God's regression aside, isn't it plausible to assume that the universe has always been here? To my way of thinking, a universe (or god) that popped into existence out of nothing is no more (or less) reasonable than one that has always been here.

Religion is adaptive

To repeat (as it bears repeating) religion is adaptive in an evolutionary sense because it increases the cohesiveness of the tribe, most especially in terms of getting tribe members to die for the tribe. That is the major reason that religion is nearly universal and the urge built into our genes. There are other reasons for its universality of course but they are secondary.

For example religion tries to explain death. It also tries to gain adherents by giving them some hope of escaping death, usually by postulating a life after death.

Religion and morality

Okay, but what about morality? Doesn't belief in God promote morality?

No, it doesn't. Again let me quote Nobel Prize-winning physicist Steven Weinberg "...on balance the moral influence of religion has been awful." He adds, "With or without religion, good people can behave well and bad people can do evil; but for good people to do evil—that takes religion."

In his book, *The Faith Instinct: How Religion Evolved and Why It Endures* (2009), Nicholas Wade argues rather convincingly that our sense of spirituality and our moral instinct have been hardwired into our brains by the evolutionary process.

But a student wrote: "Selfishness is clearly the greatest virtue if there is no one to answer to after death."

Enlightened self-interest is probably what he meant (if he really thought about it) and not "selfishness." Enlightened self-interest for social beings includes getting along with others. Stealing from people, killing them, bearing false witness, etc. for personal gain is usually a bad strategy, which is why such things are condemned in all major religions. The religious ideas come from human biology and from human experience, not from an imagined God.

Evangelicals and creationist types propose a God to dispense moral law because they instinctively know that you can't get it from watching what goes on in nature. However the laws that they dispense come from humans and therefore lack the kind of absolute authority that the Imams and the clerics would prefer. They think we children need a God to make sure we see moral truth, and of course they see themselves as God's spokespersons demonstrating again that religion is not about morality as much as it is about power.

God is beyond morality

The idea implied in the observation that tradition is valuable in helping us to decide ethical questions is a good one and one with which I strongly agree. I especially like the traditional idea that the basis of all morality is the Golden Rule: Do unto others as you would have them do unto you. We don't need a God or the baggage of some outmoded religion to see the wisdom in this.

But, to be candid, I think God is beyond morality and isn't in the business of handing out morality guidance to humans.

Spirituality

Another way of looking at this is to realize that a belief in God can be seen as part of a spiritual dimension to human existence. However I would say that belief in the sort of God that would reward mass killings with sexual fun in heaven with many virgins is not spiritual at all, but is instead a kind of bestial expression of human politics and the war system. In contrast, a desire to transcend the reality of mortal flesh is what is spiritual. David E. Comings in his book, *Did Man Create God?: Is Your Spiritual Brain at Peace with Your Thinking Brain?* (2008), demonstrates that genetically and neurologically this spirituality is what is hardwired into our brains and not a specific belief in God or gods. He writes: "Spirituality can be defined as a feeling of a connection with something greater than oneself..." (p. 530)

Spirituality is similar to religion but without the social and political baggage that all religions insist on carrying. Even in the guru system there are guru politics. I think spirituality tries to get away from the politics of religion that exist in churches, monasteries, temples, ashrams, etc. It is interesting that all major religions have a "more" spiritual expression. There is for example the Catholicism of the Pope and that of Thomas Merton. There is the Islam of the powerful in the Middle East and there is the Islam of the Sufis. There is popular Hinduism with its endless rituals and its many manifestations of God, and there is the Hinduism of the Upanishads.

God both exists and doesn't exist

God exists and if he didn't exist we'd have to invent him.

Or:

God doesn't exist and the God that people believe in is a construction of the human mind.

Both statements are true and mean the same thing.

Fulfilling God's plan?

We were not "created." We evolved. This is a very important difference. If we had been created (and designed!) we would be very different. We would not have the flaws that we have. All the evolutionary baggage that we carry: too big a head for the pelvis of women, a nearly useless appendix, a blind spot in the eye, an immune system that is often overkill so that we have allergies, sperm using the urinary tract, the war system, emotions that are counterproductive, like jealousy and hatred, etc.—all this baggage gives the lie to a divine creation in the image of God. God as a designer (one hopes) would be a bit beyond all this. And God as God from any thoughtful perspective cannot have a urinary tract or a belly button or even a digestive system. He doesn't need to be worshipped. Such ideas are those of people from the Bronze Age.

And how silly it is to talk of "fulfilling God's plan." If God has a plan that needs fulfilling, he doesn't need us to do it. The idea of a personal God who gives us free will is really a kind of social-psychological statement about humans in society. Society wants accountability; it wants people to be responsible for their actions. It wants license to punish. Free will is therefore necessary. Consequently it is necessary to have a God who stands aside and lets his creatures do their thing, so to speak.

Reincarnation and karma

What is reincarnated is self-identity, which is the same for everyone, like the candle flame. Reincarnation in the strict denotative sense cannot possibly exist since according to the Buddha all is flux and nothing stays the same including ourselves. So even if we were to miraculously come back to life in another vehicle (whatever that may mean) we would not be the same anyway. Like all great world religions, Buddhism has a lot of mumbo-jumbo that is to be imbibed by the mass mind. Apparently the Buddha did not believe in deities, but that hasn't stopped some Buddhists from believing in them.

All religions must be understood from a symbolic and psychological point of view. Their truths are seldom if ever literal.

Karma can be seen as (1) a symbolization of the evolutionary process in which the genetic endowment dictates like begets like (with variation of course); (2) literally as a sop to the masses so they can believe that evildoers will get their just deserts eventually; and (3) a reminder that everything we do has consequences, although those consequences may not manifest themselves immediately or even if they do, we may not be aware of them.

Buddhism has been greatly corrupted since the time of the Buddha, yet the core is still there and is still one of the finest guides to living ever devised. Read the *Dhammapada*. All the rest is merely commentary, some of it not so good. Zen, which incorporates insights and an essence from Taoism, is a reaction to the intellectualization of Buddhism that has grown up over the centuries.

In yoga and in Buddhism (with the exception of the highly significant Mahayana "correction" to make Buddhism more social) the idea is to get away from all of the conditioning we experience, not only the social, but the instinctive as well. The Buddha left his family behind to find enlightenment, which in other religious traditions would be morally reprehensible. (It helped that his family was very well off!)

To simplify, in the final analysis all intellectual systems, mathematical systems, systems of belief, etc. will be found to have somewhere a contradiction within them, which is why the split developed within Buddhism. We yearn to become spiritual beings, yet we are made of flesh and blood. All actions (all karmas) lead to more of the same. We are imperfect creatures in a world we do not fully understand.

Chapter Eighteen:

Aliens among Us?

You can take everything conclusively known about extraterrestrial life and fit it on the period at the end of this sentence (with room left over for about seventeen angels).

—Joel Achenbach, *Captured by Aliens: The Search for Life and Truth in a Very Large Universe* (1999), p. 33

Microbial life is probably abundant in the cosmos

Two discoveries in recent years have persuaded most scientists that life beyond earth is not just possible but likely.

First, there is the discovery of extremophiles, bacteria that live in sulfurous hot springs or deep inside the earth or at the bottom of deep oceans. Instead of deriving their energy from the sun, they are able to use heat coming from within the earth to metabolize.

Second, there is the discovery of (at last count) over four hundred planets (albeit not earth-sized planets—yet) revolving around other stars.

What the first discovery means is that life doesn't have to exist or begin in conditions such as there are or have been on the surface of the earth, but can thrive in

166

places previous thought hostile to life. That opens up a whole lot of the universe to life including parts of our solar system previously thought inimical to life, such as in an ocean under the icy crust of Europa or beneath the inhospitable surface of Mars. And the fact that planets are now clearly plentiful means that there are numerous places for life to develop.

Of course microbial life is not what we consider intelligent life, and so even though life is probably plentiful throughout the universe, intelligent life may be rare. Is it possible that we are the only intelligent life in the cosmos?

Well, as some wag asked, is there intelligent life on earth?

Rare earth?

Two authors that think intelligent life is rare are geologist Peter D. Ward and astronomer Donald Brownlee who present their case in *Rare Earth: Why Complex Life Is Uncommon in the Universe* (2000). Their subject, astrobiology, is a science still in eager anticipation of its first object of contemplation. Their thesis is that our earth is indeed rare, the product of innumerable rare events and unusual conditions, so much so that we should expect to find similar circumstances elsewhere only very rarely. Acknowledging the recent discoveries of extremophiles, single-celled organisms that can live in very harsh environments, the authors aver that microbial life on the other hand should be plentiful. They believe, nonetheless, that the leap from microbes to complex life forms is a very rare event indeed.

Their argument is based on all the things that can go wrong. They cite a formidable litany of hindrances including the need for a planet to be the right size at the right distance from a star of the right size and composition, to the need for plate tectonics (for biotic diversity and the recycling of materials) and a large moon (to stabilize the planet's tilt and temperature), to a Jupiter to sweep the system relatively free of deadly planet-crossing bodies, and especially to a very long time period in which to evolve, etc.

The miraculous not so miraculous?

Their argument is tantalizing and difficult to fault. We have only one example of the rise of complex life, and it seems reasonable to conclude that the factors that allowed this life to evolve are necessary. But I am troubled. If I look at the factors that led to my birth, my birth as exactly me, the whole process seems rather miraculous. If my parents had never met, if my mother had had a headache that night, if, in fact, she or my father had behaved in any way differently from exactly how they did behave during the time up and including my conception, another little sperm might have fertilized the egg and I would not exist. Or, take a hand at bridge. If you are dealt 13 spades, you can be pretty sure that something fishy is going on since the odds against getting exactly 13 spades are astronomical. However, the odds against being dealt any other exact hand at bridge are also astronomical; in fact the odds are identical. But some combination of cards must be dealt! So the fact that the development of complex life on this planet seems miraculous in the sense that everything had to be just right for it to develop may be a misconception. I think it's akin to the anthropic principle. If our solar system were different perhaps some other creatures would be here rhapsodizing over just how miraculous all the coincidences were that produced them!

Life as we don't know it

The authors, of course, are talking about carbon-based "life as we know it." Since it is massively difficult to speculate on life as we don't know it, especially considering that something like 95% of the universe, the so-called mysterious dark matter/dark energy, is still totally beyond our ken, they are wise to qualify the argument. I would add that life may take on forms and modes that we wouldn't recognize as being "alive." It may be, for example, that the stars are "alive." We know that they are born, they grow, reproduce and die. They spew their seeds, the heavy elements out into space where they attract other elements and form new stars. Such life would be "life as we wouldn't recognize it." There is also the possibility that life may take on forms and modes totally beyond our comprehension, giving us "life as we can't possibly know it." An example would be my friends "the energy beings" who live, reproduce and disappear in a small fraction of a nanosecond, too quick for us ever to be aware of them.

Yes, one may, I hope, speculate. Certainly that is what Ward and Brownlee are doing here. Regardless of how carefully they conform to what is currently known in a scientific sense, and regardless of how carefully those speculations are expressed, they are postulating from a sampling of one. But the authors know this. On page 282 they write, "The great danger to our thesis...is that it is a product of our lack of imagination. We assume in this book that animal life will be somehow Earth-like. We take perhaps the jingoistic stance that...lessons from Earth are not only guides but also rules." Nonetheless they say that "evidence and inference" lead them to believe that the earth is very rare indeed.

Life everywhere?

Taking a different stance is David Darling who delivers a blistering critique of the "rare earth" hypothesis in his book, *Life Everywhere: The Maverick Science of Astrobiology* (2001). He begins with the nitty-gritty problem of just how to define life. If you haven't been introduced to this strangely knotty problem, ask yourself this: do we consider reproduction, metabolism, growth, etc. in our definition? Where do we place viruses? And what about prions, which cause mad cow disease? Are they alive? And which characteristics are essential and which are not? The postmodern definition now preferred by most authorities I have read is "undergoes Darwinian evolution." Is that adequate? Is that the essence?

Next Darling recapitulates ideas about how life began. The main idea is that life may be an inevitable consequence of the nature of matter and energy. It appears that matter is self-organizing. He goes on to make the case for a universe with abundant life. But along the way he presents a rather eye-opening critique of Ward and Brownlee book mentioned above.

A creationist bias?

To my mind Darling refutes their arguments; but of course the conclusions really come down to how "rare" one thinks "rare" is. What really surprised me was how Darling shows that the arguments in "Rare Earth" may have been advanced because Ward and Brownlee were under the influence of one Guillermo Gonzalez, professor of astronomy at the University of Washington, who is a creationist with the usual supernatural agenda.

This was a bombshell to me. But Darling shows that nearly every argument that Gonzalez makes is designed (pun accidental) to discredit the idea that there is life anywhere but on earth. On page 112, Darling refers to an article entitled "Live Here or Nowhere" co-authored by Gonzalez for a publication called "Connections" published by Reasons to Believe, Inc. of Pasadena, California, whose mission is "to communicate the uniquely factual basis for belief in the Bible." The article concludes, "The fact that the sun's location is fine-tuned to permit the possibility of life—and even more precisely fine-tuned to keep the location fixed in that unique spot where life is possible—powerfully suggests divine design."

Panspermia

Brushing aside this revelation, I'd like to note that Darling argues that life forms on other worlds, however dissimilar their chemistry, are likely to be familiar to us in the sense that if there is an atmosphere, some will have wings, and if there is an ocean, some with have fins, if there is a solid ground to walk upon, some will walk and run, and if there is light to see, some with have eyes. This idea of "convergence" is dictated by the laws of physics which requires evolutionary adaptations to take forms that work efficiently within certain environments. Of course if the life forms we eventually discover exist in great dust clouds, their adaptations may be very dissimilar and surprising. Even on solid ground here on earth some run and some hop, some crawl and some slither.

Additionally, since it is now known that bacteria spores can exist more or less indefinitely (some have been revitalized after hundreds of millions of years of dormancy: see page 150), the once discredited idea of panspermia, namely that life originated elsewhere in the universe and arrived here as spores, has been rejuvenated. Personally, I've always liked this idea championed by Fred Hoyle and Chandra Wickramasinghe; however I'm convinced that life could arrive from without or develop from within. Either way (or both) seem likely to me.

The Drake equation

To continue, let's just postulate that intelligent life exists not only on earth but elsewhere. Two questions then come immediately to mind: can they (have they?) visited us and can we contact them or otherwise become aware of them?

This would involve us in the wacky world of UFOs and alien abductions on the one hand and the scientific Search for Extraterrestrial Intelligence on the other. Central to these questions is the famous query from physicist Enrico Fermi: "Where are they?" by which he meant, if intelligent life exists elsewhere in the galaxy why aren't they here by now?

Well, maybe Fermi's quip isn't as significant as he thought it was, and at any rate a more detail look at the question of do they exist? brings us to the equation made famous by Frank Drake in which the probability of extraterrestrial intelligent life existing is made mathematical.

Simply (and simplistically) put the equation states that the number of civilizations in our galaxy with which communication might be possible equals the number of stars times the fraction of those stars that have planets that could support life times the number that actually develop intelligent life times the number that develop a technology that releases detectable signals times the length of time those signals are released into space.

Interstellar travel is mostly a problem in biology

Unfortunately the equation cannot be solved because too many of the variables are unknown. For example, even though, as Fermi supposed, there has been enough time for ETs to develop the ability to communicate with us (or even to travel here!), they may not want to. For what it's worth the number Drake and his colleagues came up with in 1961 for our galaxy is 10 civilizations capable of communication.

So let me put it this way: the assumption that there is an innate propensity for life to reproduce ad infinitum is one that is hard to argue with when applied to life on earth. The assumption that life elsewhere will have a similar urge is also reasonable. However when we look at the average lifespan of species on this planet we realize that something like a million years is the norm. How much of the galaxy could a species that exists for a million years colonize? Further qualify this by asking what is the average lifespan of a species that leaves the environment to which it is adapted? It may well be that if we ourselves were to go space-faring we might find artifacts of extinct ETs but not the ETs themselves.

There is also the question of why intelligent beings would want to live in hostile environments. Some of their kind, like some of our kind, might very well volunteer for the uncertainties of a lifetime in space and a lifetime in space for their progeny, but most probably would not. And how massively advanced does a civilization have to be to go space-faring, confident that nothing will go wrong over the span of a hundred years, a thousand years, ten-thousand years...? Humans as presently constituted would find living on a spaceship for even months at a time very difficult. Think of how our ideas have changed since the time of Shakespeare, a mere four hundred years ago. By the time the space travelers are gone a generation or two, it is possible that they may change their minds about the value of the mission and want to turn around and come back.

As Freeman Dyson said, "Interstellar travel...is essentially not a problem in physics or engineering but a problem in biology." (p. 130 in Michaud, Michael A.G. *Contact with Alien Civilizations* (2007)) He might well have added "psychology."

Galactic vandalism

Another issue is that of sending out probes or self-replicating "Von Neumann machines" that would terra form the galaxy while endowing the new turf with the seed of their makers. But again, why would they? Darwinian biological creatures tend to reproduce to the carrying capacity of their environments; but any creatures that have the intelligence to colonize space would presumably be beyond such biological imperatives. In fact, the real question is why would any advanced society want to create more of its kind? It seems to me more likely that such creatures would want instead to observe life forms different from themselves in so far as possible. Michaud recalls that Andrew Clark and David Clark characterized sending out self-replicating probes as "galactic vandalism." Michaud adds that such probes could end up threatening the civilization that made them. (pp. 170-71) It's possible that sufficiently complex self-replicating machines could "evolve" into something with intentions very different from that of their creators.

There are historical examples of civilizations reigning in their exploratory and reproductive instincts, such as the Chinese before the European Age of Exploration. We might also note the declining birth rates today in industrialized countries. It may very well be that once biological creatures reach a certain level of understanding, they stop all activity because there is no desire to do anything. If we build machines that have an intelligence vastly superior to ours, unless somehow the desire to continue is built into them, why would they continue?

Life as it might be

Now we need to make a distinction between life as we know it and life as it might be. A little modesty would suggest that life as we know it might be just one way of being alive. True, our knowledge of chemistry favors carbon-based, water-based life. However because of our ignorance about dark matter and dark energy at least 95% of the universe is still a complete mystery to us. Here's a quote to end the chapter:

We don't really know what life is. We may as well try and catch the wind as pin life down with a tidy definition.
—David Grinspoon, *Lonely Planets: The Natural Philosophy of Alien Life* (2003), p. 98

Okay, one last point: possibly the most efficient and effective way of sending life from one star system to another (and developing intelligent life) is by sending bacterial spores which can remain vital for hundreds of millions of years under proper conditions such as being surrounded by some kind of medium that protects them from cosmic rays. Although it might take the spores hundreds of millions of years, maybe even billions, to evolve into intelligent life, nonetheless this might be the way life spreads in the cosmos. It might be part of our story, assuming of course that we *are* intelligent life.

Chapter Nineteen:

Pleasure, Pain and Drugs

It's all about brain chemistry, but you can't fool Mother Nature.

When I run, afterward I feel great. No doubt pleasant chemicals are coursing through my brain, but it is also the case that just relaxing physically is a pleasure. (When I am actually running it feels like my lungs are bleeding!) Normally just relaxing can be a bore, but the fact that I am physically tired makes it delicious to just sit. Often my mind is active even though my body is tired.

The point here is somewhat similar to the realization that when you stop banging your head against the wall it feels good, except with running there are no injuries (hopefully) and no painful after effects. If you had not been banging your head against the wall, your head would feel neither good nor bad. You would not notice how it felt. Most of the time I am neither tired nor not tired. It is a wash. There is no pleasure or pain either way. But after vigorous, sustained exercise, just relaxing is a pleasure. This is brain chemistry.

An eternal truth: Chickens should be two years old before you count them.

This applies to all addictions, habituations, lifestyle changes, etc. Some authorities give six months, but I'm here to advise you that this is premature. Six months without smoking is certainly a good sign, but I guarantee the cravings are still there and the possibility of backsliding is very real. I gave up smoking cigarettes decades ago but I can still recall the habitual patting of my breast pocket for the cigarette pack and the "life has no joy" feeling after dinner without a cigarette. Today nothing could tempt me back to smoking cigarettes, but I didn't feel that way after I had given them up for only six months.

Let me repeat: *It's all about brain chemistry, but you can't fool Mother Nature.*

A persistent delusion

The use of drugs to achieve happiness, joy, a sense of power, excitement, entitlement, a life without pain, etc., is one of humankind's most ancient and most persistent delusions. Mother Nature, through the evolutionary mechanism took care of such flights of fancy long ago, and still maintains an iron hold on any attempt at a circumvention. Why?

Pleasure and pleasant states of mind are part of the pleasure/pain system that the evolutionary mechanism uses to get individuals to behave in ways that are effective at staying alive and reproducing. These "rewards" have to be for behaviors that are genuinely adaptive. If Mother Nature rewarded non-adaptive or ineffective behavior her creatures would indulge in such behaviors and would eventually lose out in the evolutionary game and become extinct.

Since effective behavior that leads to the rewards is often hard work requiring knowledge and skill, individuals naturally look to ways to get the same rewards without all the work. Enter drugs—alcohol, cocaine, nicotine, speed, marijuana, opium, etc. They alter brain chemistry by mimicking the brain's and Mother Nature's own substances or inducing them. Instead of getting dopamine and such parceled out in small amounts, drugs can trigger a rush or prevent an uptake so that the high lasts longer and is more intense. The problem is that while you may have a mountain of cocaine, you have only a few tiny mini-drops of dopamine or serotonin, and after a few rushes the supply runs out, diminishing returns set in and it takes more and more dope to achieve less and less in terms of pleasure and escape from pain. And of course there's little to nothing left to reward you when you do something adaptive.

One of the reasons things work this way is that, if they didn't the doper would be lying around all the time doing his dope and sooner or later the wolves would be at the door and bye-bye doper. In fact that is what happened in the prehistory many, many times.

Parasitic and mutualistic relationships

But another reason that these mind-altering substances have a limited application is that they are the product of some other living thing trying to work some magic on us to its advantage. In the case of alcohol, the living producer is a yeast and something to ferment (wheat, grape sugar, corn, etc.); in the case of marijuana, nicotine and opium, it's just the plant. From an ecological point of view the yeast and the plants are using their chemicals to get humans to help them reproduce. They are in a sense looking to form a parasitic relationship with us—or in the long run hopefully a mutualistic one. Our natural chemistry through "diminishing returns" helps us avoid becoming a host to parasites and so works in such a way as to make the attempts of the yeast and the plants to hijack our brains ineffective.

To put it another way, we and the yeast and the plants have had a long history of interaction in which we have worked out a relationship that allows us to function effectively. Many phenotypes subject to the negative effects of alcohol have been weeded out. Some groups of people, like Native Americans and Polynesians who haven't had a lengthy experience dealing with the yeast are still struggling mightily with alcohol. And we all know people that cannabis has reduced to stoner status, and other people who find the weed nothing more than ineffective and smelly.

Beyond pleasure and pain

To go beyond pleasure and pain and become something more or different from the sort of creature we are is an ideal. This may be required if we are to survive in the long run. Creatures dominated by the polarities of pleasure and pain are easily controlled by controlling their pleasure and pain. In fact the great danger is that they will do that to themselves; that is, we will use our technology and our knowledge to increase our pleasure and minimize our pain to the exclusion of all else until we become mere protoplasm and neurons attached to machines that do the maximizing and minimizing. Only if we somehow subscribe to a higher order of value than the escape from pain and the pursuit of pleasure will we avoid that pleasure machine as our terminus.

If you concentrate on how you feel when you are feeling neither pleasure nor pain you will discover bliss.

Chapter Twenty:

Is Science True?

The authority of science comes from the power it gives humans over their environment...To think of science as the search for truth is to renew a mystical faith...

–John Gray, *Straw Dogs: Thoughts on Humans and Other Animals* (2002), p. 20

Science leads to superior results

Science, which is just common sense codified and shared, cannot come to final answers about the nature of the universe or the meaning of existence or even tell us what life is. We can learn more and more about the world around us, and we can extend our sensual, technological, and intellectual reach further and further into space and time, both forwards and backwards, both to the very, very small and to the very, very large, but never enough to reach ultimate knowledge. We are finite creatures in an infinite expanse.

What allowed science to triumph over the church and the tribe was its superior *results*. Only concrete results in the form of superior goods and services, and especially in the form of superior weapons and armaments, could defeat the tribal mind and the authoritarian clerics.

A candle in the dark

The title of Carl Sagan's book, *The Demon-Haunted World: Science as a Candle in the Dark* (1996), is both a profound description of the human world before (and without) science, and an apt metaphor for what science really means to us. In particular, Sagan refers in Chapter 7 to the world of Europe during the time of Pope Innocent VIII (was ever a personage more ironically named?) in which "perhaps hundreds of thousands, perhaps millions" of people were tortured and burned at the stake and/or dismembered or otherwise killed for being witches or for consorting with demons and other imagined agents of Satan (p. 122). Sagan wants to remind us very lucky citizens of the postmodern world just what it was like in the middle ages when the nature of truth was decided by the coercive power of authority and not by observation and evidence. Where would we be without science? is the question of the book, and Sagan's title is the startling answer. We would still be in the dark ages.

But what is this magical science that makes all the difference in the world?

It is common sense codified and repeatedly tested. Instead of accepting the existence of demons or aliens or satanic conspiracies based on reports from people, common sense asks to *see* the demons. We want proof of their existence, and we want that proof verified by others. Sagan has what he calls a "baloney detection kit" in which he has science confront new ideas. This kit includes

- "independent confirmation" of the "facts";
- the idea that "arguments from authority carry little weight";
- the possibility of falsification;
- the use of Occam's Razor.

181

We cannot have absolute certainty

Virtually everybody reading these words knows what Sagan means by these terms. The astonishing fact, and one of the key points of his book, is that the over-whelming majority of people in this country and throughout the world do not. The even more astonishing fact is that even some people with college educations are not clear about the need for evidence and independent confirmation of evidence before one can say that something is true. They also do not know that this truth is only a tentative conclusion, forever subject to being overthrown by new evidence, evidence that might arrive tomorrow.

Many people are dissatisfied with this and want absolute certainty. But what Sagan is at pains to say is that such "certainty" is never forthcoming in this world. Such certainty is the province of religion. An integral part of the human condition is to realize and accept the fact that we cannot have absolute certainty, that the best we can have is a candle in the dark, and that candle is science. Without it we have an arbitrary truth, a truth of, by, and for authority. And that kind of "truth" can hurt you if you happen not to be on the side of authority, or happen to fall out of grace with the powers that be.

Surprisingly, science is not intuitive

The question arises, why is the method and the logic of science a mystery to so many people? Sagan's answer is, it isn't taught in school. His book is an attempt to right this wrong. He would like to see the scientific method as part of our grade school curriculum, and see it continued on into college. I would add that science is not intuitive. It is not politically correct. It is politically neutral and sometimes it is amazingly anti-intuitive. People who make their living primarily with their political and intuitive (i.e., social) skills tend to be the ones most threatened and most ignorant of science.

But can science be taken in moderation? Is it possible to say that, well, we need to be scientific about most things, but there are (shall we say) "affairs of the heart" to which science has properly speaking nothing to say? Should science and religion exist forever on separate planes? Personally, like Michael Shermer, editor of the *Skeptic* magazine and author of *Science Friction: Where the Known Meets the Unknown* (2005), I am a rational skeptic and believe that science is a tool that can be applied to all of our affairs, in business and politics, history and religion, and even in choosing a mate, while recognizing that, left to our own devices, we tend to follow the scientific method willy-nilly, by starts and fits, by happenstance and sometimes only when it is thrust upon us by dire necessity.

The scientific method

A curious thing about science and the scientific method is how alien it is to a large number of humans. It wasn't until perhaps the 19th century when the technological payoffs from science began to be felt that even a significant number of people made it a point to think scientifically. Even today I occasionally run into people for whom the scientific method is a mystery. They understand the definition of the scientific method, but their minds operate in a different way. They don't see the point. They argue for some position drawing significance from authority or their inner feelings while evidence and rationality have little to no effect. We see this especially among people who for whatever reason feel compelled to hold onto to a discredited view such as the earth is not warming and if it is, man isn't causing it, or the Bible said it and so it must be true, or homosexuality is an abomination.

The method is simple enough: there is an idea or a theory or just a guess about why something happens or why something is. Then there is a methodological test of the idea with observations and experiments perhaps and a sharing of the results with other people who then give their input. Finally there are tests by others using their equipment and experience and more sharing. It is strange to say perhaps that the most common rival method is simply an appeal to authority of some kind. "It's always been done that way." "So and so said it was this way." "It is written." "This is how I feel...," etc.

Objective truth?

In the essay, "Confronting O'Brien" (that's the O'Brien of Orwell's 1984), from his book *Facing Up: Science and Its Cultural Adversaries* (2001) Steven Weinberg makes it clear where he stands on the possibility of two plus two equaling five, or on the so-called "strong" social constructionist view of scientific knowledge. The Nobel Prize-winning physicist writes that while "there is no such thing as a clear and universal 'scientific method'", nonetheless, "under the general heading of scientific method" there is "a commitment to reason...and a deference to observation and experiment," and "Above all...a respect for reality as something outside ourselves, that we explore but do not create." (p. 43)

In the chapter, "The Non-Revolution of Thomas Kuhn," Weinberg writes that "the task of science is to bring us closer and closer to objective truth." It is here that I demur. I think it would be better to say that science more and more allows us to better manipulate the environment to our advantage (or disadvantage!) and to see further into that environment—to smaller phenomena, more distant objects, and more clearly into the past and the present—rather than to speak of "objective truth," which in this context is little different from "ultimate truth," or a "final theory of everything."

The dream of "objective truth" is the dream of religion and is anathema to Weinberg's sentiments elsewhere in the book. Note, however, that he carefully writes, "closer and closer to objective truth." That's a nice qualification, but I think he should have qualified the notion of "objective truth" as well.

Finally here is mathematician Tobias Dantzig's sweeping cautionary advice to the scientist: "...he will be wise to wonder what role his mind has played in...[a] discovery, and whether the beautiful image he sees in the pool of eternity reveals the nature of this eternity, or is but a reflection of his own mind." (*Number: The Language of Science,* p. 242)

Chapter Twenty-One:

Science vs. Superstition

The struggle in the world today is between intelligence and stupidity, between knowledge and ignorance, between science and superstition. It might seem that intelligence should be a prohibitive favorite, but actually intelligence is the underdog. While knowledge is power and science has given us—at least those of us in the Western world—a relatively luxurious existence and an unprecedented life expectancy, it is merely a nouveau experiment evolutionarily speaking. For all its power, intelligence has never really been tried before on the scale that we find in humans. With our intelligence we have used the scientific method (and plenty of trial and error) to acquire vast knowledge. We have developed an immensely powerful culture which is a tool unlike anything ever seen before.

More pleasure and pain

But what is the downside? The problem with humans is that we are driven by those terrible opposites, pleasure and pain. We are enslaved by them, so that our science and technology are directed toward increasing pleasure and diminishing pain. When that is fully accomplished we will have come to a dead end. We will become brains in a vat.

Instinctively many people know this. And they know (unconsciously of course) that the only way to avoid this dead end is to reign in science. In other words, ignorance is better than knowledge, because knowledge, as Dr. Faustus learned, is intrinsically evil since we humans are not psychologically capable of being gods. We will only use our power to acquire pleasure and avoid pain. We will move closer and closer to a virtual reality with electro-chemical hookups to our bodies so that our pleasure will be maximized and our pain minimized. That is our drive.

So when conservatives seem to practice willful ignorance and to oppose progressive ideas, they are merely doing their best to (blindly) struggle against the death of the species.

There is no hope for humans as presently constituted. Our primitive brains, our passions and desires rule the rational aspects of our brains in a way little different from that of a crocodile.

Two scenarios

There are two ways that humans can overcome the terrible defect of the limbic system: we can either evolve into creatures less driven by our primitive brain modules or we can engineer those drives out of our systems. Here are two scenarios leading in that direction. The first is more biological evolution. The second is cultural evolution. Cultural evolution moves at mach speed while biological evolution creeps along. But it is unclear which will have the greater effect in the future. Here's the first scenario:

Humans trash the planet in some manner so that civilization collapses and we are returned to a more primitive state in which we fight over what remains. Out of the chaos will emerge the new humans, a bit different from the old humans. They will build a new civilization which will again collapse. This may go on for a long time in a cyclic fashion, perhaps for tens of thousands of years. During each rise and fall, just as during the advance and the retreat of the ice during the ice ages, humans will adapt and evolve. At some point humans will have changed so much that they may be wise enough to avoid the collapse of their civilization. Let's leave this scenario at this point.

In the second scenario humans merge with the products of their culture, the machines and the biologically engineered transplants, so that they are able to overcome the dictates of their limbic systems and are able to avoid trashing the planet and are able to maintain and advance their civilization. This may take only a couple of hundred years or so.

At this point both scenarios arrive at the same place, more or less. The "humans" in either case will be different from the humans living today. What happens after this?

...[T]he stomach's point of view is that the brain is the servant of the stomach to help it scrounge around for food....[But] Eventually man shall live primarily for the concerns of the brain, that is, for art and science, and all forms of culture, and the stomach shall be servant.

—Alan Watts, from *The Philosophies of Asia* (1995), p. 7

Chapter Twenty-Two:

Why We Grow Old and Die

Nothing last forever but the earth and sky

—Kansas, "Dust in the Wind"

It may come as a surprise for you to learn (I know it did for me) that science is not quite certain as to why we die. I mean generally. In each specific case a cause of death is usually made: heart attack, cancer, gunshot wound, and so on. But as far as why human beings in general die rather than go on living indefinitely, the answer is murky.

No death from "natural causes"

It used to be the case (and perhaps still is) that coroners would cite "natural causes" as the cause of the death of certain old people. However in some places this is no longer allowed since science has established that there is no such thing as the nebulous "natural causes." If the medical examiner looks closely enough it will always be found that some part or parts of the body failed for one reason or another and should be cited as the cause of death.

Some people think we die (theoretically) because it is good for the species. Some people think we die be-

189

cause it is programmed into our cells to die. Others think we die because our bodies wear out. "Senescence effector" genes in our cells are cited. We learn of "mutagenic free radicals," "shortening telomeres," "reactive oxygen species," etc. These are proximate reasons no doubt, but they do not explain why the evolutionary mechanism does not allow us to be immortal.

In a sense death is a byproduct of sexuality, we might say, noting that dividing nonsexual bacteria, for example, are theoretically immortal (as are cancer cells). Some species (salmon, for example) die immediately after reproduction. There are studies showing that such species may go on living if they do not reproduce.

A most salient point is that natural selection works most effectively when the organism is at or near sexual maturity. The further the organism gets from the onset of sexual maturity, the less effect natural selection has on making it adaptive; that is, making it healthy and effective in warding off dangers from the environment.

Put another way, what this means is that the evolutionary mechanism "cares" less about older organisms that are no longer sexually reproductive than it does about younger ones that are. Or put still another way, the harmful mutations that are selected against in younger organisms are not selected against in older individuals because those older individuals have been so few in number that the presence of their genes in the overall gene pool is small and cannot affect natural selection in a significant way. Why? Because they are drown out by the many genes from younger individuals.

From entropy to chaos to death

In another sense we can say that because most organisms much past the peak years of reproduction will die from predation, accident and natural catastrophes

such as tsunamis, hurricanes, droughts, volcano erup-
tions, broken legs, etc., it is biologically pointless and evolutionarily very difficult to evolve genes that would prevent ageing. Simply put biological evolution does not support system maintenance much past the age of reproduction. The genes that would code for system maintenance
have so little value that they are simply not selected. Notice too that genes that are detrimental to the systems of
old individuals or genes that are neutral are also not selected. Instead gene mutations are randomly selected,
that is, by accident. Since there is the second law of thermodynamics, or entropy, a random system will just run
down. It will go to chaos; and for our bodies, that means
breakdown and death.

If this is not clear, let me say that I did not understand these subtle points for a long time. Furthermore,
they seem to beg the question of why the evolutionary
mechanism does not allow organisms to continue to reproduce as they get older. The reproductive capability of
lobsters, for example, actually increases with age, and
indeed this is understood as being one reason they live
relatively long lives. So why isn't our reproductive age
unlimited?

Death is a byproduct of sexuality

The answer to this conundrum is also very subtle:
such a strategy wouldn't work for the vast majority of
sexually reproducing organisms because the species would
be static and couldn't change with the environment. The
old reproducers would, through the strength of their experience and position, dominate reproduction and naturally
work against change. Consequently, the species would
drift away from their changing environment and become
less fit. The faster the environment changes the less fit
the unchanging old reproducers become. Additionally, the

faster an environment changes the faster the species must adjust; therefore, reproduction at an earlier and earlier age would be selected for.

What all this points to is the melancholy fact that we age and die because of sexuality. Sexual reproduction only works if the young have a better chance at reproducing than the old. It should be realized that someone a generation younger is, paradoxically, a generation older in terms of genetic experience. The gene pool has mixed one more time. The young can only have the advantage if the experienced and powerful get old, weak and die. And so we do.

Sexuality fights pathogens

The next question would be why do we have to have sexuality in the first place? That question is much easier to answer. In general it is because sexuality allows for a more frequent and thorough mixing of the gene pool so that favorable suites of genes are more quickly brought to the fore and selected while detrimental combinations of genes are exposed and selected against. More specifically sexuality developed in response to the ability of disease microbes to reproduce and mutate so quickly. Sexual reproduction throws a different immune system out against potential pathogens every generation. Without the sexual mix, our immune system would be ready to respond to the microbes that have just mutated. Unfortunately those microbes just evolved to take advantage of exactly that immune system.

Afterword

I was not asked if I wanted to be brought into this world. I was not consulted. Neither were you.

Three perceived truths

1. People are animals.
2. People are stupid.
3. Life isn't fair.

Three eternal truths

In light of the three perceived truths, three eternal truths suggest themselves:

I. The world is not as we think it is.
II. Too cynical is never cynical enough.
III. Everything breaks down at the extremes.

This book has been an attempt to shed light on these eternal truths and to guide the reader to transcend them.

It must also be borne in mind that:

- There's always a dark side.
- There's always a counterculture.
- There's a reason for that.

1. People are animals

I love animals. I love cats, dogs, and all the animals of the forest and plain. I love the birds in the trees and even the fish in the sea. But animals have little to no insight into what they are doing or the ability to see much beyond the immediate present. For the most part they act out their genetically programmed roles. Sometimes they surprise us, but usually they will do what they have always done, what their kind did yesterday and the day before and a thousand years before that. These behaviors are the behaviors that have been effective and have made them who they are.

For an animal its drives are purely biological: sex and subsistence; and for social animals, adhering to the ways of the pack, the herd or the tribe. Aside from the few of us who ever invent anything new or discover something unknown, we just live out our lives as creatures of the evolutionary mechanism, getting enough to eat, moving our bowels, avoiding predators and keeping warm.

An animal, human or otherwise, does what it needs to do to survive in an everyday sense with little care for the morrow. We humans are very good at avoiding immediate disaster, at surviving on a day to day basis in a myriad of environments, from the Arctic cold to the deserts of the Middle East to the slums of Mumbai. But as the environment accelerates toward something unknown and really unknowable, can we survive with only those ancient tools?

2. People are stupid

I should also explain what I mean by "stupid." I use the term to mean willfully ignorant and mentally lazy including a tendency to accept on "faith" something that could be researched or investigated. Stupidity isn't so much a question of I.Q. as it is of attitude.

Stupidity is lethargy of the mind, a slowness to make connections, and above all, again, willful ignorance.

Additionally we are given to what psychologists call "cognitive dissonance" or what George Orwell called "double think." Simply put, we lie to ourselves and others a lot.

3. Life is unfair

As far as life being unfair, this perception is a direct result of our having a moral sense about what is right and wrong, about what should accrue to those who do good and what should happen to those who do bad.

Unfortunately the cosmos and the evolutionary mechanism care not at all about what we think is right or fair. Our morality is the morality of our kind, the morality of the tribe, and it doesn't necessarily apply to the larger world. The evolutionary mechanism only cares about what works and what doesn't. It has no favorites, gives not a whit for good intentions or for having one's heart in the right place. Good works are good works only in so far as they actually are effective in an evolutionary sense. In this regard think of the accommodations that animals and plants make with parasites. The tree harbors no moral sense that the bugs that eat its leaves are evil; instead it rewards them with nectar or other sustenance to entice them to leave the leaves alone. The mitochondria cells in our bodies were once parasites. Eons ago our cells formed a symbiotic alliance with them and they became part of the cell's machinery.

I. The world is not as we think it is

Most of this book has been an elaborate argument establishing beyond a reasonable doubt that "The world is not as we think it is" is true—in fact it is multitudinously true.

II. Too cynical is never cynical enough

This is similar to the doper's dream of that mountain of cocaine and his eventual realization that too much cocaine is never enough cocaine.

People are evolutionary creatures with desires that can never be completely satisfied. That is the way the evolutionary mechanism works: always more desire with only a brief sense of satisfaction, a temporary sense of being sated, and all too brief sense of optimism and belief in reason and goodness, fairness and justice, and then tomorrow the hunger returns and the sense that something is going to go wrong and we become overwhelmed with angst and fear and pain and suffering. As the Buddha taught, life is unsatisfactory (*dukka* is sometimes translated as "suffering" or "affliction," but it amounts to the same thing).

This is the human condition. We are the products of an evolutionary mechanism that has neither rhyme nor reason, neither purpose nor plan. The gods are all products of the human mind, fueled by desire and yearning, ignorance and superstition. We are all here as on a darkling plain where ignorant armies clash by night (Matthew Arnold), where life is a tale told by an idiot, full of sound and fury, signifying nothing (Shakespeare), where hell is other people (Sartre), and the only meaning that life can offer is that which we ourselves superimpose on it (existentialism).

Life is unsatisfactory or barely satisfactory because the evolutionary mechanism only requires that an organism be just sufficient to its environment. By that I mean the average organism is on average able to get enough to eat and reproduce. There is no genetic coding for an efficiency greater than that needed for survival and reproduction. In practice this means that the best phenotypes in favorable environments will do well, but the worst in unfavorable environments will not make it at all, and the average organism will be okay in a good environment and suffer in a bad one.

Psychologically we are happy and have good brain chemistry when things are going well in the subsistence and reproductive (i.e., "love") departments. Since we will be often struggling in those imperatives, we will find life unsatisfactory or even painful. Furthermore, organisms younger than their prime years or older will also find life not entirely agreeable, and therefore again life will be unsatisfactory or even painful.

We humans today have through our powerful culture provided for a superabundance of subsistence for most people (at least in the Western world) and most people find life worth living. But we in the developed world are living in unusual times. We are the lucky ones whose environment is highly favorable: people are fat and raise fat children. The gods are good. It is our science and technology that has enabled us to exploit the resources of the planet to give us this good life, that and our social and political organizations. But if capitalism is a ponzi scheme on the future (and as currently practiced, it is), then our superabundance will be just a brief transition period between the struggles of our ancestors and the horror to come for our descendants.

But maybe humans will learn to live within their means.

And maybe we won't.

III. Everything breaks down at the extremes

Our logic, our mathematics, our bodies...the universe itself, as I have tried to demonstrate in the book, all break down at the extremes or eventually. Period. End of story. Sayonara. Good-bye.

There is always a dark side

And there is always a counterculture, and the reason for that is that humans have to have a place to go when they are out of favor with their society. When the world was young and humans few and the planet largely unexplored, humans could walk away from the society that for whatever reason rejected or condemned them (or vice-versa). In the large city states, in the modern nation states with only the most undesirable land left unoccupied, humans have nowhere to go. So they go over to the "dark side," to the counterculture. From an evolutionary point of view that is better, much better than suicide. Incidentally, one of the reasons that forgiveness became a central tenet of Christianity is to dissuade those tribe members currently out of favor from going elsewhere or joining an opposing tribe.

No purpose, no plan

Furthermore there's no purpose, no God's plan, no goal. You are not going to wake up in some hereafter and have it all come clear. The lights *are* going to go out. And that will be that. Period. End of story. All is dust in the wind.

Okay, given a rational skeptic's point of view, given that faith is for dullards (or saints) and you are neither, given that life is a struggle and then you die, given that life really is unfair, and that the real truths behind the perceived truths are not known to us or can ever be known to us, given that the eternal truths are just the way things are, given that we are like the ants that blindly follow the pheromone trails, how do we find nirvana in this vale of tears?

If we base our behavior on a true understanding of the human condition and our biological nature unfettered by fairy tales and the bromides of politicians, hucksters, demagogues, corporate spokespersons, priests, preachers and various talking heads; if we strip ourselves of the propaganda of the commercial world and the dictates of the tribe and come to a rapprochement with our animals selves, we might, just might find that life is worth living.

Expect nothing

With these melancholy considerations in mind how do we not give in to despair? But we mustn't get depressed or give way to depression. It is better to lie to ourselves (Christianity, Islam, Judaism, Hinduism, etc.) than to lose faith in the morrow. Once we have given up hope, we are like the old guy who can't get it up anymore and thinks that that's important (Papa Hemingway) or that other old guy who finally, but finally got in on the Internet stock boom in December of 1999 and shot himself before the flowers of spring had sprung because he thought THAT was important.

So what is important, and what is the Way and the Light? How do we figure out what gets us through the night to a glorious tomorrow where the sun is shining and the birds are chirping and God's in his heaven and all is right with the world?

Basically what we do is lose our desire. Fundamentally what we do is not give a shit. Expect nothing

and never be disappointed. Expect nothing and occasionally be pleasantly surprised. Expect nothing and never
want. Live simply, modestly without ornament while
avoiding the social ramble (Satchel Paige). Eat sensibly,
drink moderately and only with meals; don't stay out late
and chase loose women (or worse, loose men), and practice
moderation in all things, including of course moderation
(which means hang one on once in a while, stay up all
night with the wind and the rain in your hair on a mountain meadow, or eat nothing for a week but spring water
and lemon juice). Believe in what is reasonable, and for
which there is evidence. Shun true believers, but make
allowance for their delusions. Respect the other guy's
point of view and always, but always remember, even
when you are absolutely certain you are right, you could
be wrong. And bet on the favorite, unless the odds are
prohibitive, or better yet don't bet at all.

Bibliography

Achenbach, Joel. *Captured by Aliens: The Search for Life and Truth in a Very Large Universe* (1999)

Austad, Steven N. *Why We Age: What Science Is Discovering about the Body's Journey Through Life* (1997)

Baldi, Pierre *The Shattered Self: The End of Natural Evolution* (2001)

Barrow, John D. *The Book of Nothing: Vacuums, Voids, and the Latest Ideas about the Origins of the Universe* (2000)

Bloom, Howard *Global Brain: The Evolution of Mass Mind from the Big Bang to the 21st Century* (2000)

Boese, Alex *Hippo Eats Dwarf: A Field Guide to Hoaxes and Other B.S.* (2006)

Brockman, John, ed. *What We Believe but Cannot Prove* (2006)

Brockman, Max, ed. *What's Next?: Dispatches on the Future of Science* (2009)

Burger, William C. *Perfect Planet, Clever Species: How Unique Are We?* (2003)

Clark, William R. *A Means to an End: The Biological Basis of Aging and Death* (1999)

Comings, David E. *Did Man Create God?: Is Your Spiritual Brain at Peace with Your Thinking Brain?* (2008)

Crick, Francis *The Astonishing Hypothesis: The Scientific Search for the Soul* (1994)

Damasio, Antonio *Looking for Spinoza: Joy, Sorrow, and the Feeling Brain* (2003)

Dantzig, Tobias *Number: The Language of Science* (1930)

Darling, David *Life Everywhere: The Maverick Science of Astrobiology* (2001)

Dawkins, Richard *The God Delusion* (2006)

_____ *The Selfish Gene* 30th Anniversary Edition (2006)

Dean, John *Conservatives without Conscience* (2006)

Easwaran, Eknath, ed. *The Upanishads* (1987)

Farrell, Warren *The Myth of Male Power: Why Men Are the Disposable Sex* (1993)

Goleman, Daniel *Emotional Intelligence* (1995)

Gray, John *Straw Dogs: Thoughts on Humans and Other Animals* (2002)

Grinspoon, David *Lonely Planets: The Natural Philosophy of Alien Life* (2003)

Harold, Franklin M. *The Way of the Cell: Molecules, Organisms and the Order of Life* (2001)

Bibliography

Hawking, Stephen *A Stubbornly Persistent Illusion* (2007)

_____ *The Theory of Everything: The Origin and Fate of the Universe* (2002)

Hayflick, Leonard. *How and Why We Age* (1994)

Horgan, John *The End of Science: Facing the Limits of Knowledge in the Twilight of the Scientific Age* (1996)

Klarsfeld, Andre and Frederic Revah. *The Biology of Death: Origins of Mortality* (2004)

Libet, Benjamin *Neurophysiology of Consciousness: Selected Papers and New Essays* (1993)

Margulis, Lynn and Eduardo Punset *Mind, Life, and Universe: Conversations with Great Scientists of Our Time* (2007)

McCrone, John *Going Inside: A Tour Round a Single Moment of Consciousness* (2001)

Michaud, Michael A.G. *Contact with Alien Civilizations* (2007)

Morris, Richard *The Big Questions: Probing the Promise and Limits of Science* (2002)

Nesse, Randolph M. and George C. Williams *Why We Get Sick: The New Science of Darwinian Medicine* (1994)

Norretranders, Tor *The User Illusion: Cutting Consciousness Down to Size* (1991, 1998)

Olshansky, S. Jay and Bruce A. Carnes *The Quest for Immortality: Science at the Frontiers of Aging* (2001)

Orwell, George *1984* (1949)

Ratey, John J. *A User's Guide to the Brain: Perception, Attention, and the Four Theaters of the Brain* (2001)

Rose, Michael R. *The Long Tomorrow: How Advances in Evolutionary Biology Can Help Us Postpone Aging* (2005)

Sagan, Carl. *The Demon-Haunted World: Science as a Candle in the Dark* (1996)

Shermer, Michael. *Science Friction: Where the Known Meets the Unknown* (2005)

Stamos, David N. *Evolution and the Big Questions* (2008)

Stenger, Victor J. *Quantum Gods: Creation, Chaos, and the Search for Cosmic Consciousness* (2009)

_____ *God: The Failed Hypothesis: How Science Shows that God Does Not Exist* (2007)

Susskind, Leonard *The Cosmic Landscape: String Theory and the Illusion of Intelligent Design* (2005)

Tavris, Carol and Eliot Aronson *Mistakes Were Made (but not by me)* (2007)

Taylor, John. *When the Clock Struck Zero: Science's Ultimate Limits* (1992)

Trefil, James. *101 Things You Don't Know about Science and No One Else Does Either* (1996)

_____ *Are We Unique? A Scientist Explores the Unparalleled Intelligence of the Human Mind* (1997)

Vacca, John *The World's 20 Greatest Unsolved Problems* (2005)

Wade, Nicholas *The Faith Instinct: How Religion Evolved and Why It Endures* (2009)

Walker, Martin G. *Life! Why We Exist... And What We Must Do to Survive* (2006)

Ward, Peter D. and Donald Brownlee *Rare Earth: Why Complex Life Is Uncommon in the Universe* (2000)

Ward, Peter D. *Future Evolution* (2001)

Watts, Alan *The Philosophies of Asia* (1995)

Weinberg, Steven *Facing Up: Science and Its Cultural Adversaries* (2001)

Wells, H. G. *The Time Machine* (1895)

Wilson, Edward O. *On Human Nature* (1978)

Wright, Robert *A Short History of Progress* (2004)

Made in the USA
Lexington, KY
25 March 2013